WHAT PEOPLE ARE SAYING ABOUT

WHEN A PAGAN PRAYS

When a Pagan Prays is a fascinating look into why and how we pray that tackles the difficult questions of Pagan prayer with eloquence. Essential reading for all Druids and any Pagan who prays or wonders how prayer fits in to modern practice.
Morgan Daimler, author of *Where the Hawthorne Grows*

In *When a Pagan Prays*, Nimue Brown has crafted an engaging, heartfelt and careful exploration of her journey toward reclaiming prayer. This book is a wonderful introduction to prayer for any spiritual seeker. It will especially appeal to those who value both rationality and spirituality and are concerned with the profound ethical questions facing the contemporary world. *When a Pagan Prays* bravely faces these challenges with an open heart and open mind.
Jamie Heckert, PhD, Integral Yoga teacher and co-editor of *Anarchism & Sexuality: Ethics, Relationships and Power*

T0163410

When a Pagan Prays

Exploring Prayer in Druidry and Beyond

When a
Pagan Prays

Exploring Prayer in Druidry and Beyond

Nimue Brown

Winchester, UK
Washington, USA

First published by Moon Books, 2014
Moon Books is an imprint of John Hunt Publishing Ltd., Laurel House, Station Approach,
Alresford, Hants, SO24 9JH, UK
office1@jhpbooks.net
www.johnhuntpublishing.com
www.moon-books.net

For distributor details and how to order please visit the 'Ordering' section on our website.

ISBN: 978 1 78279 633 6

A CIP catalogue record for this book is available from the British Library.

Design: Stuart Davies
www.stuartdaviesart.com

Printed and bound by CPI Group (UK) Ltd, Croydon, CR0 4YY

We operate a distinctive and ethical publishing philosophy in all
areas of our business, from our global network of authors to
production and worldwide distribution.

CONTENTS

Acknowledgements

Thanks as always to Tom Brown for cover art and love and making life not just possible and bearable, but also worth living. Thanks also to Trevor Greenfield, whose encouragement, support and good thinking make all manner of things possible. He is all I could ever wish for in a publisher. Thank you Bish for a catch, and Will Rathouse for an academic rescue mission. Thank you Theo Wildcroft, Talis Kimbery, Jo van der Hoeven, Jamie Heckert, Graeme Talboys, Morgan Daimler, Cat Treadwell, and Lorna Smithers, whose support, kindness and inspiration are much appreciated.

Along the way a lot of people shared thoughts with me about prayer – many in informal conversations. I didn't always get names. To anyone who has at any time paused to share a thought, about this or any other subject in person, by email, on the social networking sites or over at www.druidlife.word press.com I'd just like to say how much I appreciate this. Books are not written in a void. Books are written in communities, in the midst of life and chaos, and would not happen were it not for the kindness, interest and practical support of other people. Every book is a tribal effort, and I do not believe any author would come out with anything decent if they worked entirely alone. Books have to be for people, and because of people, or they're just an exercise in navel gazing.

Thank you, everyone.

What is Prayer?

What is prayer?

Can it be said to work in any meaningful way?

Is there a place for prayer in modern Druidry? And, conversely, can you call anything a religion if it does not have a prayer practice within it?

What can we Druids learn from prayer practice in other religious traditions?

This is the story of what happened when a somewhat agnostic Druid took an academic interest in prayer, and then found that approach wasn't going to work.

Chapter One

Making Introductions

I have come to the conclusion that *When a Pagan Prays* isn't really a book. It is two books that have somehow managed to occupy the same space. One of those books is an amateur attempt at some academic writing, featuring comparative religious studies, psychology, sociology and a bit of research. The other book is an experiential tale of what happened to me when I started to explore prayer as a personal practice. Of course there are areas of overlap between the personal and the theoretical. The book I planned was the first one, the exercise in comparative religion, which turned out not to be enough. Prayer doesn't make sense as an abstract subject. It's left me with some challenges in the redrafting because I want to preserve as best I can the sense of the journey that occurred while I was writing. I think it also worth flagging up that what this book turns into is not quite what it seems to be in the first chapters.

While I usually start non-fiction books with a clear plan, I seldom end up with anything I had anticipated. The process of writing a book is a journey in itself and the destination of the final page not always obvious. Even when I think I have it all figured out, I often prove myself wrong. In the stages of trying to write coherent bits of text, ideas come together and I see things I'd not thought of before. This was perhaps least true of my first book, *Druidry and Meditation*, where I mostly did follow the original plan. So dramatic were my realisations during the first draft of *Druidry and the Ancestors* that I had to step away for a second period of research before I could finish it. *Spirituality without Structure* was at least small enough that I could keep it on a leash. This book stopped and started several times, evolving in unexpected ways as I tried to get it onto the paper. I write this introduction having completed a book that has surprised me repeatedly. That's been rather a lot of fun, and has taken me on a powerful journey.

You could read this book as an inspirational true life account with a passably happy ending. You could take it as the intellectual exploration with self as case study I originally intended. You could probably follow it as a workbook if you feel sufficiently inclined that way. There aren't many "how to's" in here. I am not offering instant transformation, or salvation or any of that claptrap. If the idea of Druidry, of Paganism, or of prayer interests you, then wander along with me through a journey of ideas and experiments that took me to some interesting places.

What is Paganism?

For me, Paganism is a blanket term covering a great many paths. The commonality in Pagan paths is that these are traditions that honour the natural world, and hold the individual responsible for a personal, spiritual journey. Paganism includes polytheism, duotheism, monotheism, pantheism and animism, and there are atheists who identify with Pagan traditions, too. It is not a religious cluster based on esoteric belief, but on recognition of the values of ancestry, nature, and old religions. Magic is often innate to Pagan practice, not necessarily in a spell-making sense, sometimes more about recognising the innately magical aspects of existence.

I self-identify as a Pagan because I honour nature and my ancestors, I am influenced by tradition, and walking my own path. I am a maybeist, in that I have no idea about ultimate truths of life, deity and eternity. I think we humans make a lot of guesses on this, some of which may be right.

What is Druidry?

I'm a modern Druid. While I find inspiration in what little I know about the ancient Celts, and mediaeval literature, I do not claim to do anything authentically historical. If you want Druid history, I recommend Ronald Hutton's *Blood and Mistletoe*. It's also important to note that there are many different forms of modern Druidry. I am not representative of what all Druids do. I was trained by OBOD (the Order of Bards, Ovates and Druids), but am feral in my instincts, experimental and unruly. It is fair to say that I have an on-going relationship with OBOD, but that does not mean my writings are a good representation of the rest of the Order. I've written for The Druid Network and Henge of Keltria as well, and I do not speak for them, either.

I have a deep fondness for the crazy and often fraudulent characters of the Druid revival period and am the founder of a largely tongue-in-cheek Secret Order of Steampunk Druids (neither secret nor orderly). I've also been involved in other, more sensible things too, including the recently establish Auroch Grove. I am serious about play, frivolous in the face of authority; I tidy up chaos and disarray structures. Other Druid authors, at Moon Books and beyond, offer very different takes on what it means to be a Druid. I am not authority, just one voice in a vast, complex and ever evolving conversation.

Bearing all of that in mind, all I can offer you to be going along with is a personal, working explanation of what I think Druidry means. (Enough caveats?) This is individual, not definitive: *Druidry is a spiritual dedication to seeking knowledge and developing skills and creativity for the good of your land and community.*

There are a lot of extra things an individual can add to that about gods, ancestors, sacred inspiration, the kinds of service undertaken, the nature of their dedication and more. I will recognise anyone as walking a Druid path if they are working this way, regardless of how they see themselves. I won't insult anyone by putting that definition onto them, either. In much the same way, a person who lives minimally, peacefully and mindfully can be understood by Jains as walking the Jain path. What we do is really of far greater importance than the words we attach to our efforts.

Druidry is vast, and very much shaped by the individual practising it. We each walk our own path.

This is not a "How to be a Druid" book. There are no instructions to follow that will turn you into a Druid. Part of being a Druid, as I see it, is that you have to figure out your own way of doing things, based on your own understanding, your place, time, the needs of land and tribe, your gifts and inclinations. What I can offer you are ideas to chew over and accept or reject. I can share what I've done, and you can copy that if you want, improve on it, create a variation that works better for you, or carefully head off in another direction. There are no wrong answers. If this is your first book on Druidry, all I can say is... I wouldn't have started here. However, you shouldn't have any trouble following the ideas. This book was written more for those people who know their awens from their... elbows, but I welcome all comers and hope you find something useful in the mix.

What is Prayer?

Here is another personal and working definition: *Prayer is something that people do as a manifestation of religion or as part of a spiritual practice.*

Beyond that, it is remarkably difficult to pin down, being a term for a vast array of activities. Prayer crops up in religions across the globe, but what exactly it is, and how it works, depends a lot on who is doing it in what context, and why. Prayer runs the full gamut from insidious control method to means of enlightenment. I've tried to unpick how some of that works.

As with most things, what you get out of prayer depends a great deal on what you bring. The reason you undertake prayer is going to influence what happens to you. If you are a love-drenched tree-hugging pacifist, your prayers will probably be full of love and light and at the very least, more feel-good affirmations. If you are a person in pain, or full of anxiety, you'll pray differently, but that's no less meaningful. People coming to prayer out of curiosity, a desire for mystery, a hunger for connection, can do all kinds of good work. If, on the other hand, you are a fascist control freak with a desire to torture puppies, you aren't going the enlightenment route this week and the experience of prayer will probably just reflect your own fantasies back at you.

Mostly what we bring to prayer, is us. Mostly what we do in prayer, is us. If we want to reach out to the cosmos, or some aspect of it in an honourable way, we'll do that thing. If we want to justify our own greed and bullshit, prayer is a tool to be used.

Dear God, I'm good!

If you are intent on being self-important, are deaf to all criticism and blind to the suffering of others, prayer will not help you much. You get what you bring. If you are willing and able to be open, vulnerable, listening, if you are here to be changed, that's a very realistic possible outcome, no matter which tradition you follow or the methods you adopt.

Talking about Gods

Inevitably, the subject of gods comes up in this book rather a lot. I've tried to be passably consistent in my language use, but it might help to flag this before we get going.

> **God:** I use this word when I'm talking about ideas that relate to monotheistic traditions, where there is only one god, and where this concept of singularity matters when considering an issue.
>
> **Gods:** I use this one when talking about more polytheistic traditions. I've not put "or goddesses" after each instance for simplicity, but please hear that as being what I mean. For me, the gods may be any or no gender.
>
> **Deity and divinity:** I like these words because they express a

sort of being/energy/possibility without pining down numbers, genders, where exactly it can be assumed to exist, and so forth. Whenever it is feasible to do so, I default to these terms.

The divine: That which defies language. Is that one being, many beings, the universe itself? I don't know, and that's rather the point. I'll use this interchangeably with deity and divinity where possible.

Spirit: Might or might not be the same as deity, but pertains much more to the world as we experience it. That which is sacred and also present and available, I tend to describe as spirit.

Religion: For me a religion is a formal social structure with functions that can be understood entirely in social and psychological terms.

Spirituality: Is a process of actively engaging with spirit/divinity. This can happen in the context of a religion, but is neither dependent on religion, nor an inevitable consequence of it.

Atheism: A firm belief in the non-existence of deity that furthermore considers theistic belief to be ridiculous, dangerous or otherwise ill advised.

Nontheism: A non-dogmatic belief that deity does not exist. Nontheists are able to accept or tolerate theists. An animist whose belief in manifest spirit does not have room for gods in it, or a person who believes there may be some larger divine force that is beyond us and therefore irrelevant, might effectively be a nontheist in that their practice holds no reference to deity.

Chapter Two

Considering the Nature of Prayer

When I first started thinking about prayer, it was very much from a position of intellectual curiosity. In many ways, my prompt was Alain du Bottan's *Religion for Atheists*, which explores the social benefits of religious activity. Prayer was notable in its absence from the book. However, the idea of considering religions in terms of what they do in this world, appealed to me. While I am not an atheist, I'm not very good at belief either. In many ways the atheist position seems too much like certainty to me, but nonetheless I find a lot of atheist thinking appealing. Demanding that things make sense on their own, immediate terms rather than with reference to unknowable, ineffable plans, is something I have to agree with. Looking for rational approaches to religion led me to write *Spirituality without Structure* in one of the gaps while this book was being wrestled into submission.

There isn't really a fixed modern tradition of Druid prayer. Some groups and Orders have defined approaches to praying, but my impression is that the majority do not. Early conversations on the subject indicated to me that many Druids feel uneasy about what they see as being a practice we can only borrow from other religions. Petitioning the gods for things feels both pointless and wrong. Looking further afield, I found that people generally take prayer to mean petition, unless they are deeply involved with a spiritual path that includes a more involved understanding of the subject. This seems to be true of people of all religions.

My thinking at this stage was: other religions use prayer extensively and apparently we don't. Why is that? Are there good reasons to reject prayer, or are we missing a trick? I admit that I thought the question could just be tackled intellectually. Being the sort of person who defaults in all things to getting a book on the subject, I set off to read around.

When I was first looking for books to read about prayer, I poked about online and in bookshops. Books of prayers are plentiful, but not what I wanted. Books that consider prayer as a process are relatively few, although I did eventually track down some excellent ones, and you'll see scattered references as we progress.

In a Christian bookshop, a generous woman spoke to me about her own prayer practice. She viewed the urge towards prayer as innate to the human condition. She also found me some books, and did not blink too much when the subject of Druidry came up. "I pray to God as if I was talking to my father. He is my father. I can go to him and ask him for things," was the gist of her description. I did not learn her name, but remain grateful for her help. She spoke to me about prayer as something intrinsic and natural, and found it odd I should want a book examining how and why we pray. The shortage of such books suggests that many religious people would agree with her perspective.

From that first book (*How to Pray*, John Pritchard) a new way of thinking about the idea of prayer began to open up before me.

"Essentially it is about entering a mystery, not getting a result."[1]

I found this resonant. The author is an Anglican Christian, but the sentiment struck me as being totally compatible with Druidry as I practise it.

My next read was a Catholic book (*Ways of Praying*, John C Edwards) by which time it had become plain to me that in some quarters, prayers of petition are considered to be the least important form of prayer, at least by the people for whom praying is a professional and serious business. After that, my reading took me into works from other traditions and I wondered if I would be writing a comparative religion text. However, that would have largely been a rehashing of other people's work, and I'm not convinced the world really needs something like that.

I had considered surveying the modern Druid community in a more formal way to deepen my understanding of what we do and how we do things. However, my initial enquiries had raised the issue that a significant percentage of the Druids I had talked to were not praying at all. There are some who admit to occasional petitions, and several groups with much more involved approaches. I could get figures for the praying and not praying, I could ask nosey questions about who people pray to, and what they think they get out of it, but how much would that help? This was my first inkling that intellectual research might not be able to shed enough light on the subject. It could easily be like scraping the paint off pictures and weighing it to make judgments about the value of art works. That leaves the anecdotal, and self-reporting, neither of which constitute good science – not even in softer subjects like psychology. I don't have the kit to study what happens inside people's brains when they pray.

Why was I fearful of writing a spiritual book about a spiritual subject? It was a question I did not know how to ask myself at the time, but looking back it seems significant.

Most of my Druidry is pragmatic and not about belief. The sun and moon are real. We live and die. I bleed and eat. My Druidry is absolutely rooted in the life I live. As previously remarked, I am not naturally inclined towards belief. When I first came to this subject, I did not pray (aside from petitions thrown out to anything that would listen in times of desperation). The trouble with prayer is that it suggests belief in something and an expectation of supernatural intervention. Both made me uncomfortable.

While I have always been happy to accept that there might be deities, I had no sense of relationship with any such being, and no sense that I could pray specifically to anything or anyone. I also had no idea why or how to pray, because I do not believe that petition works. I had come to this subject, fascinated by what other people do, and wanting to stand outside of all of that, and observe. It did not take me long to realise that to have any hope of understanding what people do when they pray, how it works, whether it works and all of that, I would have to try it. This in turn required me to be open to possibilities I did not believe in, and to make a leap into the dark.

One thing I do believe, despite my bookish tendencies, is that Druidry should be at least as experiential as it is academic. I needed to walk my talk with this one. That decision was not easily made. I stalled for a while and considered not exploring this aspect of spiritual life at all. The desire to know won out in the end.

As far as I can tell, prayer is central to most religious practices. Even Buddhists and Jains do it, without envisaging an intervening deity at all. There are a great many practical consequences of prayer. These are easily discernible, and readily described so I feel fairly confident in pointing those features out. The ephemeral, spiritual aspects can only be tested by doing, but I can share what I have on that score.

Prayer practices are numerous and diverse, from the deeply private, to the public ritual, from the ancient prayer poem to the sudden improvisation. A little reading around about different faiths left me clear that there are many ways of doing it, and that individual preferences and needs are probably the best guide in picking ways of working. After all, if you feel silly, uncomfortable or fraudulent then the odds of having a meaningful spiritual experience are slim.

I've put "Druid" in the subtitle of this book because I am a Druid and that informs what I do and how I think. I think much of what I've written would apply equally to other Pagans as well, and also to non-Pagans. What I want to be clear about is that this is not a rule book for Druids. I don't believe in dogma and "should" when it comes to prayer. There are a couple of points along the way that I feel need handling in specific ways, but most spirituality is personal. What matters most is that the things you do make sense to you, and add to your life in some way. What I'm offering is a mix of things discovered through reading, contemplation and experimentation. My aim is to provide a way into the subject and a framework for considering it, allowing you to go on new and different journeys.

Given the lack of prominence formal prayer has in Druidry, this is not, perhaps, the most obvious way to start learning about Druidry. I cannot even suggest that this book will introduce you to a selection of conventional modern Druidic practices. At the same time, I feel that anything undertaken in the spirit of Druidry will bring valuable learning and insight. If you are determined and interested, it won't matter a great deal where you start.

I started at the edge of sleep, because that's always been where I do my deepest spiritual work. In the past, my focus has been meditation and the quest for lucid dreaming. I find that the borderlands of sleep, at both the start and the end of the day, lend themselves to a different kind of consciousness. I am capable of wholly different thought processes at this time. There are also practical advantages in that I tend to be warm, relaxed, quiet, and unlikely to be interrupted.

When I started thinking about prayer, I took my wondering into my pre-sleep time and just contemplated. Who or what should I be praying to? How should I pray? What should I pray for? Could I really expect any kind of results? I didn't have any answers and none of my reading gave me clarity on any of these points. People of faith seemed to know what they were doing and reported, sometimes, profound effects from prayer. Those whose faith does not include an expectation of God getting back in person, focused on the importance of doing the job well, and seemed satisfied by that even when the going was hard for them.

With their thinking supported by belief systems, people with faith offer statements like, "If God is real, we must pray. We are not asked to enjoy it, only to do it."[2] This didn't help me because I did not start from the idea of there being a deity who could possibly care whether I prayed to them or not.

"Prayer is assumed to be a normal human activity."[3] When that was the default assumption underpinning a book, I felt myself very alienated, outside of the whole thing and unable to see a way into it. Prayer, for me, has not been innate, or natural, or necessary, or any of those other things that religious people happily assert it should be. Religious people can talk about prayer as "a primary religious obligation"[4] but, as there is no Pagan structure to tell me I must pray, this is meaningless.

I don't want a structure that tells me what I must do. That is, for me, totally at odds with what it means to be a Pagan. I don't want to go through the motions of required religious behaviour working only on a belief that I should, or that it will be good for me in ways I do not understand and never get to see. For me, that seems like insanity, control, or both. I don't want either.

Looking back I can see that at this point in the journey, two important things were happening to me. Firstly, the dogmatic demand to pray because we must, and for no other reason than that it is apparently in the rules for many religions, started to make me angry. I resented it. It felt like a fraudulent and ridiculous process entangled with all the worst excesses of irrational and controlling religious thinking. The second process was the recognition that for me as a Pagan, prayer, like anything else, must stand or fall on its own merits.

I've come to think of this as the nontheist test. If a religious or spiritual practice works on its own merits, then you could, in theory, persuade a nontheist to take it up. Could a nontheist pray? I'm not a confirmed nontheist, but at the same time, I am too much the rationalist to take on trust an activity that does not seem to do anything. I became more intent, as a consequence, on understanding what praying does to people. If anything.

Most religions assume the existence of a deity who actively wants you to check in with them on a regular basis, through the medium of prayer. Offering up prayers of praise, gratitude and confession are part of the world view in which a relationship between human and divine is clearly defined. This positions prayer as a vital aspect of religious life. It also creates a framework for the social functions of prayer, which I'll explore in detail later. Druidry does not have this world view or this structure. We do not have a defined, single relationship between Druids and deity and therefore we cannot have a single, coherent duty of prayer hardwired into what we do. There is no Big Book of Everything You Need To Know About How To Be a Druid. This means we do not get a social cohesion effect by all doing exactly the same things. Again, this means what we do with prayer has to be different from what other religions are doing. Part of the point, in Druidry, is to figure things out for ourselves and take responsibility for our own practices.

Across all the Pagan traditions, there's not much definition of the relationship between humans and deity. Not all Pagans believe in personified deity anyway. Pagan deities are often aspects of the natural world. Is it likely that any Pagan deity would want to hear from me? I assume those more associated with civilization (figures like Thoth, Ogmios, Athena, Bridget) would be more open to human approach, but even so, why should I assume they want to be bothered by me?

When Druids undertake ritual, we don't order spirits or ancestors into the circle. We don't assume the gods are going to put in an appearance. Instead, we greet whatever is there and express our openness. Prayer is a form of ritual. A Druid prayer cannot, I think, start by demanding the attention of someone we do not have a relationship with. We can run up to a friend in the street and ask them to lend us some money, but we don't do that with total strangers. This is no different.

Some people experience deity seeking them and affecting their lives. I would imagine this makes it a lot easier to enter dialogue with said entity. We might turn to the gods associated with the land we live on, the things we do, or the kinds of people we are. That all creates a degree of relationship on which we might productively build. I had nothing I felt confident about drawing on. There were deities I honoured by name in my youth, but the last decade or so has taken me away from that, and I have lost all sense of connection there. Much of it, I had felt when looking back, was rooted in a desire to connect, rather than in actual, trustworthy experience.

I took to lying in the darkness, quietly saying, *"Well, here I am, if anyone wants to talk to me."* No one did. Night after night I made variation on that same, quiet, offering of self, to no discernible effect.

There are no genuine spiritual practices that offer instant gratification. It took me years to develop and deepen my meditation skills. It took me years to build confidence in ritual practice. I did not expect instant results from prayer. Curiously, New Age writing on the subject does seem to suggest much quicker results, while writers from serious religions suggest that a lack of result is only to be expected and that we aren't in it for us. And then there are the people who sell religion and prayer as an instant cure for every ill, and they worry me a lot.

Although I didn't entirely recognise it at the time, I had made a transition. I had gone from being someone who does not pray, to being a person with a regular prayer practice.

"Anybody there?"

Silence.

"Hello?"

Silence.

I kept reading whatever I could find about prayer in other traditions. I wrestled with the possibility that my own incapacity for faith would make it impossible for me to do anything productive with prayer. I also discovered the potential problem that my desire to get something concrete would make any answer I did get inherently suspect.

How could I tell if I was achieving anything with this nightly cautious attempt at sort of praying to no one in particular about nothing specific? If I did get results, how would I distinguish them from coincidences, or my own mind supplying the voice of God in an act of self-indulgence?

Chapter Three

To Whom Do We Pray?

For Pagans and Druids, our religion does not automatically define a focus of prayer for us. In monotheistic faiths, this issue does not exist. There is only one god and your religion will give you a name for it. For those working with a polytheistic understanding, it may just be a case of deciding which deity most resonates with you or makes most sense at the time. You may have a pantheon of preference to work with. It may also be the case of seeing which deity comes to you. Relationship with deity is not necessarily a one-sided thing and prayer is not necessarily a one-way process. Animists tend to think in terms of spirit, and can have entirely different perceptions of deity from polytheists. An animist approach to prayer is necessarily going to be a bit different again. Then there's the nontheist question. What does a nontheist pray to?

Anyone who entertains for a moment the idea that prayers may be answered, has to consider the implications of being heard: namely the attention of a deity. A person who is not open to being changed by that encounter may find prayer difficult, if not impossible.

Prayer is, in essence, an attempt at starting a conversation with something. There are many possible answers to consider here. I don't think any are more right than any other – different people at different times may need to come at this in different ways.

We may be talking to ourselves. That might be in the sense of our most literal, actual being, or some "higher self". Prayer in this context is a form of meditation and inner conflict resolution.

We may be talking to something imaginary. If all we are interested in is the effect of the process of prayer, then the reality or unreality of the recipient may be irrelevant. We might change ourselves by prayer with no reference to external sources, imaginary or otherwise.

We may be praying to a force or intelligence outside ourselves. They may or may not hear. They may or may not respond and we may or may not be able to tell if we got a response, and may or may not be equal to interpreting it if we did get something.

The questions of what we mean to achieve and who we mean to talk to are closely connected. What power do we ascribe to whoever we are addressing? Do we see them as all-knowing and all-powerful? If we do, then we also have to work out why prayers go unanswered, or why we even need to mention our requests in the first place. Surely they know what we want already? Standard answers to this include ideas of our being insufficiently good and devout to get a response, our having asked for the wrong thing, our not being able to see what the grand plan is, or having been given instead something we didn't know we needed. Life is frequently challenging and painful. If we imagine a wholly benevolent god who loves us personally, this can be hard to square with the manifest failure of many petition prayers. Starving children continue to die. Innocent victims of disasters are not saved. Terrible things happen to good people. The exams, operations, interviews and accidents we pray to survive, do not always go well for us.

It is very hard to hold together the idea of an all knowing, all powerful and wholly benevolent deity without having to include the idea of some big plan we don't know about. It may be necessary to believe that the gods hurt us for our own good, like strict parents disciplining a child. Except that the discipline seems to be handed out randomly and unfairly. We do have a lot of scope to learn and grow in the face of challenges. Are the gods kindest to us when they are cruellest? I do not know.

The reason for undertaking any action is a desire to create

change. The change we think we may get by praying might well depend a lot on whom, or what we imagine we are talking to...

Dear God, let me get through this and I promise I'll reform and be a much better person. The prayer of fear and self-preservation, offered up to a god we can bargain with. A god we can bribe and who, in his or her optimism, will forget how often that's been said before, and reneged upon.

In some cultures, old and new, sacrifice has been a form of bartering with gods. *I am killing this chicken for you. Please give me a good harvest this year.* I think this whole approach positions your deity as a super-parent figure, able to bestow and withhold favours, but potentially vulnerable to pester power.

Forgive me God, for I have sinned. This postulates a deity of unconditional love, who will see the good in us, no matter the magnitude of our mistakes and deliberate crimes. Many religions construct sins that do no actual harm, but are supposed offences against a deity who will then be fine about it when you say sorry. God the counsellor, god the shrink, always ready to hear why you are sorry, and want to do better, but never actually requiring you to get off your backside and actually improve. Gods of not actually making any changes at all, but assuaging your guilt as you go.

I praise you, God, I love you and honour you. Have mercy upon me. We envisage the dark and vengeful gods who must be appeased with sacrifices and a bit of grovelling. Gods with egos so fragile that they need us to keep saying how great they are. Gods who may smite us if we don't do a good enough job of bigging them up.

Dear God, please can I have a pony. God the provider of unearned success, shortcuts and quick fixes. God who smoothes the way and grants material wishes. The God of ego boost and self-importance who affirms our belief that our success in the world must be proof of our innate excellence. We are beloved of God.

The way in which we pray expresses a lot about our understanding of deity. Our prayers probably reveal far more about the human in the equation than the implicated deity. Ideas about gods are often projections of human need and desire. When you look at the list above, it has far more to do with human characteristics than anything divine. These are not even especially admirable characteristics, yet the way in which we pray suggests that collectively, this is often what we understand "god" to mean. We bring our greatest shortcomings to our concept of divinity. There are other ways of praying and other things to pray for that imply a completely different kind of deity.

As Druids we need to do more than project our foibles into the ether in the hopes of seeing affirming reflections of ourselves. What makes all of this more complicated is that while some of us are polytheists, we also have animist, shamanic and nontheist Druids. I choose to maintain a bias in favour of tools that can work for everyone, regardless of belief. The nontheist test demonstrates that a spiritual practice is powerful enough to work to some degree without belief being necessary. Doubt and uncertainty are key aspects of my path. In no aspect of my life do I accept the possibility of being perfectly right. There is always room to do better and room to be wrong. My understanding of everything is a work in progress, and always will be. Whatever I think today, I have to give myself room for something different to occur to me tomorrow. Therefore I never get too comfortable about anything, and especially not things for which I have no evidence at all.

How can a person come to the practice of prayer without absolute conviction that they are praying to something that exists; be that deity, spirit, or ancestor? Prayer suggests that someone or something should hear what is offered. How can a person open a dialogue in this way without believing there is something out there capable of hearing and responding? I ran headlong into this conflict as soon as I started attempting to pray.

I had no idea who, or what, to address myself to, and no sense of a dependable god-reality based on a fixed religion, to tap into. A part of me longs for the consoling, all-loving uber-parent god who makes everything lovely, even as another part of me is repelled by the idea. Neither impulse proves anything.

I believe that everything in life has a spiritual dimension to it, and I know there are plenty of scientifically verified things like atoms and radio waves that I cannot personally perceive. I am happy to accept that things I have no direct experience of exist. I've never been to Australia, but I'm pretty sure it's out there. Other people offer personal experience of deity as proof, just as they offer photos of Australia. It interests me that I am susceptible to consensus reality. Everyone believes in Australia, therefore it exists. Not everyone believes in heaven, therefore it might not. Of course I can go to Australia and check if I get the urge. Arguably I can also check out the afterlife, but that seems like a one-way ticket, and I'm not ready for that yet.

What do I know about Australia, really? Photographs and other people's words. Images from the television. I do not know what it smells like, or what it means to walk along a beach there, or feel the sun under that sky. There is a lot of difference between knowing something as a fact, or accepting it as consensus, and experiencing it. There is a qualitative issue in the kinds of experience we have. Knowing that people believe in a god is not the same as believing in a god. Knowing that some people think they have encountered goddesses is not the same as encountering goddesses. That which comes to us purely as information is not the same as that which we find by living it. Perhaps there are some people who are wholly satisfied by other people's stories and explanations, for whom the idea that someone once heard the voice of deity is enough to get them signed up to a belief system. I am not one of those people. Very few Pagans are. There is simply no substitute for first-hand experience.

After a while I came to the conclusion that my lack of firm

belief might not be a major problem. I do not have a strong belief in the existence of deities, but equally, I do not have a strong belief in their non-existence, either. I decided I could work with both my uncertainty and the possibilities this creates. I felt that because I wasn't searching for too particular an experience, I would be less likely to bias my experience with desire. Either I would find something, or not. Whatever happened, I decided that I would continue to hold my uncertainty, because that is an essential part of what I do. An experience, after all, does not guarantee its own meaning and there are many ways of interpreting spiritual experiences.

For many people, I think deities are a means of making some kind of sense of life, the universe, and everything. The idea of gods creates an impression of there being a meaning. This is not, I suspect, a meaning that most religious people could pin down, more the reassuring sense that it all makes sense to *someone*. The score is being kept. Good deeds and bad ones will be reckoned up later. Debts will eventually be paid. There is a grand plan, even if we can't figure it out. That kind of thinking can make life less intimidating, I assume.

I dabbled in existentialism in my late teens, and as a consequence lost all ability to believe in the idea of ultimate meaning. The presence or absence of gods changes nothing for me in that regard. If gods exist, it is as part of a rich, diverse and complex universe. If there are no gods, then my vision of everything is no less meaningful to me. The only meanings are the ones we make for ourselves. If gods have meanings, those belong only to them.

I have no doubt that a quest for meaning could provide a focus for prayer. For someone who seeks meaning, prayer could be quite pragmatic work. Over the years, the big question of "What does it all ultimately mean?" has ceased to interest me. I don't have an answer and I no longer believe one is available. We can speculate and formulate beliefs, but not having certainty about the meaning of life is intrinsic to the human condition.

This is an uncertainty I have made my peace with. I'd rather ask, "What can I do with this?" "What would be good?" and, "How do I live well?" We could side-track into a huge philosophical argument about how to even define "good" but that, like most things, turns out to be rather subjective as soon as you try to pin it down. Good for whom?

Atheist writers take a lot of issue with the ways in which faith in deity and dependence on prayer impact on the "real world".

"Belief in the full efficacy of prayer, for instance, becomes an emphatically public concern the moment it is actually put into practice: the moment a surgeon lays down his worldly instruments and attempts to suture his patients with prayer."[5]

However, none of the religious books that fell into my hands during the research stage advocated prayer as a cure-all. Most books tended to offer ideas along the lines of, "You do not say benevolent magic or living prayer instead of doing things."[6] This from a book that did explicitly claim that petition prayers work. I have no doubt that the kind of "religious" person who can describe rape babies as part of god's plan might also be willing to avoid practical solutions in favour of trying to pray their way through. Such an approach stems from a desire to get results without making an effort. This is not a religious idea so much as a political-economic one. Something for nothing goes with making money out of money markets and off the backs of other people's labour. Something for nothing is the mind-set of exploitation and no religion, in its core writing, actually supports this idea. Many of our world religions denigrate greed and materialism, and actively encourage altruism and good work done with the hands. See previous comments about defining the word "good". However, religions also attract interpreters who bring the something-for-nothing philosophy with them, often to justify their own success and lack of altruism.

"By their fruits shall ye know them," is one of my favourite Jesus quotes. Where religions promote responsible behaviour and actual spirituality, you don't tend to hear about people failing to do what is needful whilst waiting for god to intervene. Cults that encourage passivity, that will blame individuals for spiritual shortcomings to explain why prayers go unanswered, and that do indeed give the atheists much to grumble about, are often all about money and power. Organisations that use religion to accumulate wealth and enforce authority need to be distinguished from spiritual practices. What does a religion achieve? If the answer is that its hierarchy has a lot of money and political power, then you know what you are dealing with. Even then, it is important to differentiate between the genuine devotions of the individual and the corporate project.

Prayer is inherently political. Whether you use prayer in preference to the scalpel, the psychiatrist, the drugs, or another world view, it will be part of your place in the world. The scalpel, the psychiatrist and the drugs have their political and economic dimensions too. As with all of the things in this life that we might choose to explore, what prayer does depends a lot on what we decide to do with it. The drugs won't magically fix us either, if we don't have viable lifestyles. The psychiatrist cannot help us much if we are too paranoid to be honest. As for the faith we may put in the benevolence, omniscience and omnipotence of politicians, the less said about that, the better.

Much of human activity depends upon faith and trust. We trust our bosses to pay us and our schools not to mess up our kids. We trust that the water is safe to drink and we put our faith in the scientists who get closest to telling us what we wanted to hear. To give up faith entirely, we would have to let go of marriage. All love depends upon faith. We would not be able to put our lives in the hands of doctors: we know they are fallible, but we have faith in them nonetheless. We believe in democracy, flawed though it usually is. There aren't many absolutes in this life. An unshakeable absence of faith seems as irrational to me as a total conviction that has no evidence to support it. There is always the potential for something else. At which point, as Zen Buddhist teacher Thich Nhat Hanh says, "why not pray?"[7] If we do it with an awareness of what it might or might not be, it is unlikely to imperil our material selves in the way that atheists fear.

Those two ideas – who we are praying to, and what we are praying for – are points I'll keep coming back to. The further question of why we might pray intertwines with the two. Who you are praying to informs what you might pray for, but your reason for doing it absolutely defines it. What is it that we want? There were many things in my life that I wanted when I started to explore prayer. I didn't want any of those things to fall into my lap, unearned, because that would have felt unreal and undeserved. I need to be able to own my successes and to feel responsible for my own life. Loss of autonomy, or feeling that you have no power, is not a good experience. Of course no one has total control over their lives, but the person whose every wish was granted might be the least powerful amongst us. They would have nothing of their own. What we all need are opportunities, scenarios that are not impossible to get through and situations where "lose" is not the only possible outcome. Most often, what success or failure depends on, is our willingness to keep striving. The person who does not give up and isn't dead yet, also isn't beaten. Prayer can be a way of firming up the psyche so as to be able to keep going. That doesn't depend on getting answers or intervention.

Mostly what motivated me to start praying regularly, was curiosity. As much as anything else, I wondered how the practice would change me. We are what we do. Our activities and thoughts shape our minds and bodies alike. Would prayer practice make me more or less inclined to believe? As I started by quietly calling "Hello" into the void, what I might, or might not come to believe in remained to be seen.

It was while I was reading Thich Nhat Hanh's *The Energy of*

Prayer that I moved from academic interest, towards a willingness to experiment. That question, "why not pray?" offered an appealing challenge. More importantly, the author himself seems more focused on how praying affects the individual than what the gods might do for us. The discipline of the individual is a key part of the process. "When love and compassion are present in us, and we send them outwards, then that is truly prayer."[8]

I started examining my own thoughts and feelings, considering the place of these virtues in my life, and how I might better develop them. Contemplating how to manifest care and compassion became part of my pre-sleep, meditation time. There are only so many nights you can spend just going "Hello?" before the failure of that to achieve anything takes its toll. So, rather than look for external feedback for my noise on the ether, I started a much more practical process of trying to change myself. It seemed sensible, which the first attempt never had. I let go of something that had never made sense to me, and was at odds with my nature, moving towards something that offered more intuitive coherence. I would pray, not to see if deity existed, but simply to change myself and move towards upholding more of the qualities I would like to possess. It required no belief. My only problem at this stage was uncertainty as to how that kind of prayer was really any different from meditating.

> When we don't have the strength of the practice in us, then there is little or no strength that can come to us from outside... we are not just handing this desire over to the Buddha. We are gathering our strength from within and combining it with the strength that lies outside us.[9]

I still had no idea what "outside" meant for me. I came to understand, however, that one of the functions of prayer in the Buddhist tradition is to break down the separation between inside and outside. Where does God live? Everywhere. Divinity is inside us as well as outside. As I think that spirit is in all things, why not speak to spirit as I find it, and see what ensues? In Thich Nhat Hanh's Vietnamese Buddhist tradition, prayers can be made to spirits, ancestors and even to the living. This third option really excited me when I read it.

What would happen if I prayed to another human being? Why would I do that? Perhaps if I had no means of direct communication and things I needed to express, it would make sense. I talk to trees and to other non-human beings. Is that any different from prayer? The difference may mostly be semantic, because for me, there is nothing un-sacred about merely talking.

I've used the strange, magical time on the edge of sleep for most of my life. This is an innately private, personal space in which I have often imagined things I wanted to say to people. Impossible conversations with the dead. Times of seeking forgiveness. Sacrifices and offerings I have also made. Looking back at that now, I see how close that often came to prayer. I still do it now, making spontaneous and desperate requests to people I cannot reach. *Hear me. Give me a chance. Let me try. Don't damn me utterly. Stop doing this to me.* A hopeless, painful litany. It may not have got me anywhere, but at least it allows me to vent emotions that might otherwise cut me to ribbons from within.

Coming back to the second draft of this book, and reading the above words, written more than six months ago, I am jolted by the enormity of change. I remember being there, but it feels like a lifetime ago. I'll risk disrupting the flow to observe that much of the blame, criticism and misery finally went away. Perhaps the biggest change between then and now, is that I am clear in myself that I was put through things that were unfair and undeserved. Criticism that cut me to the core seems, in hindsight, ill-founded and irrational. I survived until it stopped, and that was enough.

I changed. I ceased to be someone who experimented with prayer and became someone using prayer as part of a daily practice. The answer to "Why pray?" became more complex: to see what happens and to work on changing myself, to open my heart and increasingly, to seek peace within myself.

At this point, my reading took me into Shinto. This is a religion that I feel has a lot in common with Druidry. There is no book, it is non-dogmatic, diverse, of the land and honours both ancestors and spirits of place. The importance of shrines in Shinto creates plenty of practical differences from modern Druidry. The spirits particularly honoured in Shinto are called Kami. They are benevolent beings, for the greater part, and tend to promote harmony. There are chaotic and destructive exceptions though. A life well lived in the Shinto tradition is a life lived in harmony with the Kami. In many ways, Kami are nature spirits, to define them in more familiar Western terms. I think it may be closer though to say that Kami are inherent in nature and that Shinto does not view people as being separate from the natural world. Therefore, to be in harmony with the Kami is, really speaking, to be in harmony with everything else that is capable of such a state.

Much of Shinto prayer manifests in the form of highly specified rituals undertaken at shrines. However, Motohisa Yamakage says, "The right way of prayer is to pay respect to Kami, as if your yearning feeling for Kami flows from the bottom of your soul."

While I've read comparable statements from numerous different faiths, something about the precise tone and language of this one appealed to me. The western language of gods and deities has so much cultural baggage attached to it that they are an uncomfortably heavy set of words to work with. I've used them for writing for the sake of familiarity, but they do not sit well with me. The influence of monotheism means that even mentioning god, divinity or deity in a Pagan context seems to require statements of clarification. Using those words brings in unwanted connotations. I've tried to resist the urge to get bogged down in defining what we mean with those pieces of language. That is partly for the sake of my own sanity, partly because I don't really know, and partly to leave room for whatever you, dear readers, bring with you. I don't think it's my job to define God(s).

"Spirit" is an awkward word too. It can be used interchangeably with ghost, essence, soul, alcohol or supernatural being. Spirit is a hard word to use precisely; again it has too many connotations that I don't really want to bring into play, and cannot avoid.

Kami immediately struck me as being both a lovely and a useful sort of word. I have no Japanese ancestry, have never been to Japan and have no experience of Shinto, which for me means the word has no baggage adhered to it. I am conscious of potential issues around pick-and-mix religion, and cultural appropriation. However, I had been sorely in need of a word. My inability to find a focus, a name to invoke or a sense of where to direct myself, had been a real block to exploring prayer. Kami is such a pleasing sound as well. Soft and resonant, even uttering it feels meaningful to me.

"Kami's light beams inside your heart and mind," Yamakage announces, as the consequence of prayer. Through daily periods of introspection, the soul is purified and grace is received. This is not a reference to the western concepts of grace or purity, but instead describes a sense of wholeness, wellness and connection to the world. Here again Shinto manifests ideas that I think have a lot of relevance for modern Druidry. At the time of reading Yamakage's words, I was wracked by depression and anxiety. My whole being had long cried out for just the kind of transformation he describes. The suggestion that prayer might be able to help me to reclaim my lost sense of wholeness and connection gave the process a deeply personal aspect.

I look back and see that as another critical moment of change. For a long time prior to then, I had carried wounds in my heart and psyche, and seen them as deserved punishments. Locked into my self-blame, I had not sought healing or even imagined myself capable of wholeness. That began to change.

New Age writing uses all kinds of language to talk about the world beyond our perceptions. Angels and devas seem particularly popular. I dabble in New Age texts, largely to know what is going on there, because I am curious about everything, but I don't identify with it much. However, Wendy Stokes' *Lightworkers' Circle Guide*[10] gave me some useful tools for approaching my difficulties around prayer. She talks about defining the nature of the kind of entity you want to work with. Rather than trying to find names and personifications to call upon, she suggests thinking about what the entities do, and calling to that. It is an approach that allows intent to define who or what you pray to. For someone in a position of uncertainty, with no relationship to, or faith in a specific deity, this has potential.

In terms of petition prayer, Wendy Stokes' approach suggests first uncovering the essence of what it is that you want. *Please can I have a pony?* does not suggest the existence of a benevolent deity devoted to handing out ponies. In this approach, what you ask for raises immediate questions about how on earth that is supposed to come to you. For the petition to even make sense, it has to be within the gift of the one petitioned. This suggests to me that we need to be thinking in terms of virtues, not assets.

All experience of the world we live in makes it clear that if there are deities, they do not exist for the sole purpose of making life easy for humans. I refuse to accept that the materially spoilt "elite" are deserving of what they get and that there's some kind of spiritual justification for starving, brutalised child victims of war and tyranny. I cannot work with a perspective in which worldly wealth is taken to be a measurement of spiritual development or divine favour. Nothing I have ever seen supports that view. Rather, I suspect that greed and cruelty are more likely to help you achieve material success, while a generous heart and an inclination towards spirituality is unlikely to bring a person huge financial reward. I also reject the idea that the life we get is somehow pre-earned or pre-defined.

For me, the idea of petitioning spiritual beings with a view to making material gains, seems wholly illogical. In desperation, facing hunger, or homelessness for example, a cry for help to anything that might listen is just human. In our most troubled moments, we will often try things that we don't normally believe in, both morally and spiritually. To appeal to spirit for more than we need, is a very different issue. I have seen New Age writers advocate prayer for anything you want, including worldly success, but I think for Druids that makes no sense at all. Asking deity to step in all the time and help with our smallest and most mundane of problems also seems disrespectful to me.

I started a new round of working, adding to that habit of offering my "Hello" by addressing it to the Kami.

Hello Kami, spirits of peace and harmony.

I remembered some of the Christian works I had read, which described prayer as being a process of making yourself available to the divine.

Hello Kami, if you are there. I am here. I am interested. I would like to be an influence for peace and harmony in the world. I would like to serve peace.

For the first time since I started praying, I had a sense that something happened. Just occasionally I would get the feeling that I wasn't throwing futile words into a void anymore. Something was listening.

Chapter Four

Prayer Does Not Work

The atheist argument against all forms of religious undertaking is simply that religion does not work. What is normally meant by this is that religions do not produce tangible, real-world effects someone could test in a laboratory. Neither do poets. Put most poets in a laboratory and you'd learn very little about what inspiration is, where it comes from, or how it functions. Much of the human experience is unpredictable and a bit irrational. Part of my problem with this aspect of the atheist debate, is that the definition of effectiveness by which atheists tend to judge religions does not tend to include the actual intentions of the religion. We also need to consider what religions do in terms of social functioning, in wholly un-supernatural ways.

Petition prayers do not work. Petitioning governments doesn't work a lot of the time either, but we still do that, too. When this kind of petition (to God or public servant) is "answered" with the outcome a person wanted, it can be easy to ascribe that to divine influence. Equally you might call it coincidence, or luck, random chance, or put it down to your own efforts. If you pray and write a letter to your politicians and something changes, you have no proof of which bit of the process did the work, and the normal, rational response is to put it down to the letter writing. Even that may be irrational. Does your letter make a difference? Or was it some feedback from the media that had nothing to do with you? We don't know. I think I've heard more heartbroken stories of prayers unanswered than I have tales of miracle cures, and people being plucked from the jaws of doom.

I have seen a lot of writing that claims prayer can improve medical outcomes, and I find that easy to accept. There's the good old placebo effect for a start. Positive outlooks, hope and determination affect outcomes in most situations. If you think that you are even a little bit helped and protected, that alone might give you the means to keep going and survive. The person who can figure out what they want such that they are able to pray for it, has clarified their ideas and focused their intent. The person who has vented their feelings through prayer has experienced catharsis and may feel better just for that. These things help for reasons that are at least in part psychological. It strikes me as being more important that there is utility in the process, than what, exactly, the mechanisms are. I am confident, however, that humans can benefit from belief and spiritual practice without there needing to be any divine intervention. However, we can also do ourselves a lot of harm.

It is possible to think about private, personal prayer in terms of how the mind functions. Prayer is a way of focusing the mind and reflecting on inner turmoil. Christian author John Pritchard points out that prayer is, "a reminder that none of us is self-sufficient."[11] Recognising the need for help and asking others to come to our aid isn't easy. We have to own our vulnerability and insufficiency before we can seek help. Arguably, formatting need as prayer and offering it to a god is a form of rehearsal, after which it might be easier to take that need to another human being. In recognising our own need, we can become more open to the idea that no one else is self-sufficient either. Perhaps if we knew that everyone else was praying for help too, it would be easier to seek, offer and accept it.

Beverley and Brian Clack in *The Philosophy of Religion* are very much inclined to see prayer as an internal process that works without needing the feedback of obvious divine influence. "Prayer then has nothing to do with influencing the outcome of events and everything to do with reflecting upon the character and purpose of our lives." Also, they state, "Religion is not a speculative explanation of the nature of the world, but a way of reflecting upon our human condition and improving our moral and spiritual sensibility."[12] This is said in the context of having previously defined prayer as being the essence of religion.

Considering prayer from a Druid perspective, I think it can be understood as a practical tool that may enable people to tackle their issues, think about their lives, seek help and also offer it. In much the same way that divination can be a more theatrical kind of counselling, apparent spiritual activities can be used to encourage mental peace and balance. I'm a big fan of using whichever tools turn out to work, and I think we do ourselves a disservice if we overlook the pragmatic aspects of those things which religions do.

My own experience of more deliberate petition prayer dates back to my time as a student with the Order of Bards, Ovates and Druids. There was encouragement to offer up petition prayer for those around us. I have no idea if any of that worked in the sense of bringing other people benefit, but there was a discernible impact on my own thinking. As a consequence of this kind of petitioning, I started to pay more attention to people around me. Not just people I knew, but strangers on the street who looked sad, or troubled, ill or otherwise suffering. I think the primary function of praying for others is that it can make us more sensitive to the needs and concerns of said others. That may lead to our taking action to help. However, if we put all our faith in prayer, and do nothing, then the odds are that nothing changes. The habit of paying attention is valuable, and is a natural consequence of praying for other people. It encourages us to look outside ourselves, which is a good thing.

There is scope here for petition to be a force for good, if we use it as a prompt to become the intervention we have prayed for. We can far more easily use prayer to assuage guilt, and as a substitute for action, something I'll come back to later in the chapter on the ethics of prayer.

I have found in my own prayer practice that petitions are an easy place to start. When I settle to pray, I first draw on meditation techniques to centre myself and quieten my mind, but to progress from there to trying to approach something outside of me requires a mental shift. In that process of trying to settle myself, I tend to become aware of anything troubling me; body tension, anxiety and so forth. Suppression is of no help, but investing time in acknowledging my own problems helps me to feel calmer about them. This gives me space to think about solutions, and to recognise where I need help from someone else. Only with the noise of my troubles dealt with can I hope to tackle anything deeper. Petition, without any assumption of response, simply helps me to clear my mind. I expect nothing, and usually get nothing, but formulating petition prayers enables me to let go a bit. It works in much the same way as sharing your woes with a sympathetic friend might. Even if no solutions are forthcoming, the process of recognition and release helps lighten the load, and keeps things in perspective. Just pinning the problems down is useful work.

Both Catholic and Jewish traditions work with confession in prayer. Here, one offers up sins to God, repenting and seeking forgiveness. From a more psychological perspective, this is only going to work for you if you invest some belief in it. If you truly feel that admitting failings and wrongdoings to God gets you forgiveness, the process will help you feel better about yourself. Whether or not this is a good thing, is an entirely different question. How much guilt should a person feel? So much of it depends on your time, place and culture as well as the nature of your transgression. The opinion of your neighbour may be a greater consideration than the words in the official book, where this matter is concerned. Needless guilt can be soul-destroying, and religions can encourage us to feel guilty about a lot of things that pertain to our natural, animal selves. Releasing that guilt is good. Feeling shame over acts that harm others is also good, but only if it stops us from repeating the offense. In that context, belief in forgiveness may be highly counterproductive.

Having a defined structure in which to explore personal shortcoming and to acknowledge to yourself how flawed you are, is likely to confer benefits. On the whole, our culture of blame and litigation discourages people from taking responsibility when things go wrong. To err is human. To learn and grow, it is essential to be able to make mistakes. We can only learn from the mistakes we make if we recognise them. Prayer is a tool for contemplating the self. Offering up our flaws may be effective as a tool for personal growth. Or it may keep us beating ourselves up.

As Druids we should not, at any point, be seeking forgiveness from anyone other than the entity we have harmed. Honour demands that we try to achieve restorative justice where we can, atoning for our failures with meaningful action. We best express repentance by doing better. Then we might stand before whatever we hold sacred, not seeking to be forgiven, but able to forgive ourselves for being human.

Prayer serves a number of social functions, which I'm going to explore in depth in a later chapter. At this point, I think it is important to just consider that the impact of prayer can be thought of in social terms, with its role in community cohesion and as a tool of authority highly significant. What we pray for informs what we might undertake to do. If a community prays openly for something, that community reinforces any behaviour which upholds the prayer. We can consider the impact of whole groups praying for peace together. We can also consider what happens to communities where collective prayers seek to change the course of political decisions with the aim of hurting minorities. Cultural attitudes can be shaped by public prayer and in that sense prayer can be very effective indeed. How we view that effect will depend entirely on whether we agree with the agenda.

The aim of spiritually minded prayer, in all traditions, is to bring the one who prays into contact with the divine. Assessing whether prayer "works" on these terms is difficult because it comes down to personal experience. The aim is to create a moment that is "a means for the believer to draw closer to God,"[13] If you imagine that someone is listening, the act of praying is one of coming into contact with divinity. "Prayer is personal and direct communication with our creator."[14]

If you pray as though you are talking to God, this may well encourage you to feel spiritual. This again is a definite effect of prayer that has nothing to do with whether anyone is listening. Being the person who prays, and feeling that deity listens, can become a narcissistic process. As with most human endeavours, what we get is going to depend on what we bring. The person who comes to prayer seeking self-aggrandisement, justifications and an ego boost, will find that. The person who wants an excuse not to act will have their easy way out. I do not think it is fair or wise to abandon any spiritual practice just because it can be misused. Anything can be misused. We have to look at our own motives and how we use our own experiences.

Observations would suggest that the gods do not punish those who use religion for their own malevolent or selfish ends. At least, not in this life. It is possible to believe in deity without thinking that the gods exist to keep score of human activities. I do not personally think deity is in the business of handing out praise or punishment. We also do not need deity to do that. We become the consequences of our thoughts and actions. It is my belief that ultimately this provides its own rewards or punishments, from a spiritual perspective.

The muttering of a few familiar prayers does not suggest drama. However, it is important to think about what the implications of prayer must be, assuming there is something out there to pray to. Are you willing to put yourself before whatever you pray to? Are you ready to open your soul to something vast and powerful that may defy comprehension? Do you want to be overwhelmed by the numinous so that it fills your heart and mind? Could you look at that, even for a moment, without risking insanity?

It occurred to me very early in the process that few things would be more terrifying than getting a response to those tentative hellos. That which inspires awe is, by definition, awful. I am too small, too fragile, to look upon any kind of enormity and not shatter. I could not afford to have real, actual deity respond with a cheerful "Yes?" to my questioning. I rather assume that would have killed me, with shock and terror. We are finite beings with limited perceptions and there are places we just can't go. There are things we cannot do without undergoing a lot of preparation first. I undertook a practice with the growing awareness that success would be deeply problematic for me. I needed to do it and at the same time I needed it not to work – which was an interesting paradox. Looking back I see how I have changed and grown through the process, no longer so brittle that I risk shattering entirely.

One of the conclusions that I came to, is that much of the time, the failure of prayer is actually a good thing. It enables us to stay sane. Only when we have minds and realities flexible and strong enough to bear contact, do we want prayer to work for us. The border between religion and insanity is a hazy one, at the best of times.

Monotheistic faiths deal with the impossible enormity of their One True God by getting smaller and more approachable figures into the mix. Jesus and Mary, saints, prophets, angels, founders and teachers all serve to mediate between the human and divine. These are people (or people-ish beings) that you can talk to, who are closer to deity than you, but not so enormous themselves as to be intimidating. The only viable way I can think of for talking to ultimate deity, depends on assuming it won't notice you.

Polytheistic faiths are a lot easier on the mind, as are religions offering spirits, ancestors or other plurality. Little mysteries are a lot more manageable. I can think about them without fear of my reason bleeding out through my ears. I might be able to touch a little mystery and not burn up entirely. I might come back from that experience a poet, not a madwoman.

Somewhere inside many prayers is a second, secret prayer that approximates to *please do not bestow all your attention on me, though. Thank you!*

As soon as I started taking prayer seriously as a process, I became nervous about it. I did not feel ready or able to stand before divinity. Or kneel, for that matter. I did not know how to be in that space and the mere idea of it frightened me. This rather begged the question of why I kept doing it. The answer is that I was used to being afraid. If I allowed fear to stop me at that time in my life, I would have achieved nothing. Most days I would not have made it out of the bed. I had learned how to push past my own fear, and how to accept it and act anyway. Day by day I kept making the choice to come back to prayer practice, trying to work out how to be able to place myself before the divine. Regardless of whether or not "divine" is just an idea in my head. I had read many books by that point and had come to consider that experiencing divinity a little bit might be both possible and desirable. I wanted to know if I could do it, and what would happen if I did. There was also the driving force of a desperate need to have more inner peace than I then possessed. I was already living on the edge of mental breakdown. Awareness of that made be both more cautious and more willing; another paradox that I learned to navigate.

Nothing I had read helped me at this stage of my journey. Modern Christian writers assume the existence of a benevolent deity who will be kind to you. The idea of god as pure love is widespread, and common in books about prayer. My sense of the divine comes to me from the natural world. Nature can be wild, dangerous, destructive, and heartbreakingly beautiful. I did not, and still do not, see any reason to expect deity to mean total love and safety. How could gods of this world possibly be that way? I find this world unpredictable, and frequently hostile. Why should the gods be different? Nothing in the prayer books I had read gave me any idea about how to pray to gods who might not be wholly friendly.

Again, I found myself returning to the idea of Kami. The Kami are individual spirits, small enough to belong to a specific place. Some of them were humans once. A being on that scale might not break me. I also considered the issue that these are beings devoted to peace and harmony. If there are many faces to the divine, some of them must be gentler. Some more benevolent and bearable entity might permit me awareness of it. I wanted the affirmation of experiencing sacredness and something outside myself, but I also had no idea what I was looking for, or doing. I am uncertain in my philosophy, but there is a hunger in me for something more, something spiritual.

I noticed changes in myself as my practice altered. Working in a meditative state, I learned to be open, vulnerable and trusting. *Here I am, Gods, please don't break me.* That has had knock-on effects in my human relationships, too. I'm aware of generally becoming more able to open up and trust.

Ever since studying a few modules of psychology at degree level, I've had a fascination with trying to observe and understand my own mental states. I think about everything, and that means I also think about how I think, which can all get a bit self-referential. However, I am the only case study available to me. While it is generally accepted in psychology that anything based on self-reporting from individuals is of limited use, I'm not writing a scientific paper and therefore suspect I can get away with it. To be on the safe side, I do not assume anything happening inside my head is universal (I'm sure that was the problem with Freud). Offering what happens inside my head gives a point of reference for anyone else who wants to go and play with the contents of their own mind. The option remains of taking my observations on trust, but there's no requirement to do so. What follows is an explanation of what happens with my mind in and around prayer.

In the normal scheme of things, I go through several discernible shifts of consciousness between being fully awake and fully asleep. The first stage is a transition from a busy, wakeful mind to something calmer, parallel to the initial settling of my body. I stop thinking about the day's events and what I should be doing next, and my mind begins to wander in less linear ways, if left undirected. This calmer state allows prayer and meditation – both of which are impossible with a busy mind. If instead I allow myself to fix on fears and anxieties, I return to a wakeful state. If I enter into meditation, the calm deepens and my thinking becomes more fluid and conceptual, less wordy.

A second shift comes, which feels perversely like a rush of energy and alertness, but as this is frequently the last thing I remember, it must be taking me closer to sleep. Sometimes I slip between wakefulness and dreaming at this time, in disorientating ways that challenge my sense of what is real.

I can use meditation to shift from wakefulness into a sleep-ready calm. If I meditate when I'm not aiming to fall asleep, I still begin with this same shift into a calm and coherent mental state with corresponding physical repose. From there, I may proceed into much deeper work – visualisation and pathworking, attempts at journeying and so forth. This deeper form of meditation causes another consciousness shift, away from the concerns of the wakeful mind and also distinct from the natural process of moving towards sleep. This is very much the trance state. Once I have entered this trance state, I cease to be aware of either my body or my surroundings. I can do this at other times, but it is much easier along the edges of sleep. My awareness is entirely elsewhere at this point. My thinking is focused and deliberate, but can also acquire a jumping sort of dream logic.

In a normal pre-sleep state, my thoughts are calm, free

ranging, and slowing towards unconsciousness. In meditation, my focus and awareness of my own thinking can be heightened. I exist to myself only within lines of deliberate thinking when I am in this state. My self-awareness changes, either becoming intensely fixed on some aspect I am exploring, or almost entirely disappearing as I become engrossed in experience.

As a consequence of these things, when I came to prayer I noticed a different state of consciousness was occurring. I pass through the same calming, pre-sleep, pre-meditation phase into a period of settledness. Once I begin to pray, my thoughts are focused as they are in meditation. If I sustain prayer – something I am not always able to do – my inner state shifts. It is discernibly different to both pre-sleep and trance states. I experience it often in a very literal sense as being in light. So literal is this that the first few times it happened, I opened my eyes to see where the light was coming from, only to find myself in actual darkness. The light I experience in a prayer state tends towards reds and golds, but I've experienced all colours at different times. The experience of being in light is soothing to me. I do not experience this as a "light of god", more as a shift in consciousness, and a journey into a space from which, or in which, sacred experience might be possible.

My brain does something different when I am praying. I experience differently. I can see how this experience might, in its own right, be understood as experiencing the divine, but I do not feel that's what is happening. I understand this as a mental shift, different from but comparable to the shift that happens when meditating. I think it is the beginning of the journey, not the end point.

Over time, I have found that I can experience intense darkness during prayer as well as light. The darkness is equally an opening to the sacred, and while it has a different feeling to the light, it is no less affirming. Despite my feelings that nature gods must have the same potential for being dangerous as natural beings, this space seems innately safe to me. I acknowledge this is possibly because the space only exists inside my own mind, or as a function of something happening with my own brain chemistry.

John Michael Greer's inspiring book *Mystery Teachings from the Living Earth* introduced me to the idea of The Law of Planes. Greer explores the way in which matter, thought, energy and emotion can be seen as discreet but interconnected planes of existence, all equally real and only able to influence each other at specific points of intersection. I could not move the pen I wrote these words with by the power of my mind alone, but my mind working through my body moves the pen to ultimately transfer ideas from inside my head, to yours. If I had tried to beam those thoughts to you, it would, at best, be considerably less effective as a method. My beaming skills are frankly not what they might be. Using the right plane of existence to get the job done, is vital. "If the thing you need to change is on the mental level, changing things on the physical level is not going to do the trick."[15] Greer takes these ideas further in a fascinating exploration of how magic works. I found myself pondering other spiritual implications as well.

Sacredness happening on a plane of sacredness would be a simple idea to insert into the model. Where is that? Do we find sacredness somewhere in the body? In the spleen perhaps? Is sacredness a state of mental discipline? Or an emotional condition? What does it mean to have a spiritual experience? Where in our planes of existence does that take place?

People of all paths talk about encountering the numinous, but in informal discussions it tends to be identified in a "you know when it happens" way. Being me, I find that hard to accept. I tend to assume that everything can be unpicked and understood. After all, if the experience of sacredness is, by its nature, beyond understanding, then it can only happen in response to things I have no control over. I do not wish to be a passive recipient. On reflection, long periods of having largely been an open-minded, passive recipient had not resulted in much numinous experience. It doesn't come to me. I do better when I actively seek it.

Christians talk sometimes about a state of grace, and about being in that state. Being outside that tradition, I must admit to not really knowing what is meant by those words. However, I like the idea of a spiritual state of being. Could a person actively choose to enter into a state of sacredness? Not a place of automatic unity with the divine, or anything so ambitious, but a state of experiencing sacredness as a deliberately chosen level of consciousness? I like this idea because it does not call for belief. You can, I feel certain, experience sacredness without having to believe in any kind of deity at all. Sacredness is a condition of being that could belong to almost anything, and does not require deity. With my uncertainty, a state of sacredness would be a good deal more accessible than attempting to bother gods I am not entirely able to believe in.

Something happens inside me, sometimes, when I pray. I am choosing to understand that as a state of, or experience of, sacredness.

I wonder if this is what prayer traditions have been striving for all along. It may be that I have merely reinvented the wheel. I wonder sometimes if the structured use of prayer in religions as a thing you do (regardless of actual effects) because it officially "works" may be a degeneration from using it deliberately to enter a more ecstatic state, the state of sacredness.

I have sat in churches enough times, while people around me repeated shared prayer formulae. No one, including the priest, has ever given me the impression they were having a meaningful spiritual experience through doing that. I've used prayers in Druid rituals, too, and while they have some interesting social effects, no participant has ever suggested to me that their consciousness was changed by praying in that particular way.

When I started learning to meditate, many years ago, it took me time and effort to achieve a deeper sort of trance state. With practice, I became much more able to trance deeply, and it took far less effort. As I've worked with prayer, I have observed a similar development. The more I do it, the more that prayer state, that being in a place of sacredness, becomes easier to attain. This has enabled me to start exploring prayer in more diverse situations. I've come to realise that what happens to me in prayer is the same as what hits me in moments of encountering the numinous by other means. Seeing wild cranes in flight takes me briefly, in an uncontrolled way, into that state of being. I find it in moments of profound and soulful intimacy, in rushes of inspiration and other moments of connection.

Would it be possible to learn how to manage that shift of consciousness into the sacred plane? Further, could that be then integrated into normal life? Would it be too much; is that sense of sacredness only manageable in small doses? Where does that consciousness of the sacred lead? Is it an end point, or a step on a journey? Can I go further with prayer, or have I reached the limits now?

Petition prayer does not appear to work. We certainly don't get what we ask for most of the time. If the gods give us what we need, beyond our own ability to perceive that, much less understand it... we may as well still say that petition prayer does not work and leave it at that. Even petition prayers that get no results are achieving something, though. This process of praying can change ideas, feelings, expectations and ways of thinking, with or without divine involvement. The act of praying creates change. It can bring about altered mental states, if you go into it wholeheartedly, engaging emotionally and intellectually. Half-hearted repetitions of barely considered words, mumbled in a state of embarrassment, aren't going to create much change.

I am finding that prayer does work, but not in any of the ways I might have anticipated. The more work I do in this area, the less interesting the idea of petition prayer seems. I expect I shall still make desperate pleas in times of crisis, but that's more of a reflex action than an expression of considered intent. The more I pray, the more attracted I become to the process and experience of prayer – not as something undertaken to further a goal or seek achievement, but as a way of shifting my own consciousness. Prayer becomes an experience in its own right, not a means to an end.

Having started the previous chapter with the idea that prayer suggests an object of prayer or something that hears, I've turned entirely the other way. It now makes more sense to me to think of prayer as a state of being, a state of mind, heart and spirit, rather than a specific intent to do something.

In some traditions, I have discovered, a person is expected to have very specific intentions regarding the effect of prayer. In Islam, prayer "requires concentration of the mind, humility and complete submission of the heart to the Almighty Allah."[16] I think that if praying requires complete submission to deity, then achieving that submission is also the point of prayer. There is a distinct difference between being open to, or experiencing the divine, and total submission to the will of another. Submission to deity might be seen as similar to the dissolving of the ego-self sought after by those practising Buddhism.

It is interesting to ask whether a person in prayer is capable of total submission to deity, especially where the words and habits of a whole culture are employed to facilitate that process. How much of what is submitted to in this scenario, is purely a human construct? Are we submitting to the idea of deity, rather than an immanent actuality of deity? When we surrender any part of the prayer process into the hands of another human being, we run the risk of submitting not to sacredness, but to human error and human greed. Prayer should be innately personal, or else it can so easily be made to serve another purpose. There have been too many prayers for the deaths of the enemy, the destruction of unbelievers and the smiting of those who we did not understand or had come to fear. When prayer becomes a political tool or the means to manipulate, it ceases to be a meaningful spiritual activity, but may remain dangerously effective as a way of controlling people.

The use of prayer in praise of deity is another widespread consideration. I have commented already that I struggle with the idea of frail-egoed deity in constant need of positive feedback from its creation. However, I think praise may turn out to have other functions. "The act of calling, "Hello?" into the void and developing it into something more like, "Hello spirits of peace and harmony," suggests a possibility to me." I am not doing this to offer praise or to get something from deity in reward for praise. I am doing it to try to become aware of that deity. The more I reflect upon these kinds of qualities, the more attuned I become to them and therefore the more open I may be to such energies.

Monotheism seems to be a relatively recent idea for humans, although the idea of one ultimate being reflected through many forms of divinity has been with us for a long time. We use names to call upon gods, but these names can turn out to be older words for titles. The Hari in Hari Krishna just means "god". Madonna simply means "my lady". Baal just means "lord". When it comes to pinning down the deity you want to talk to, names may not be all that useful where qualities may be more reliable. I wonder, therefore, if the praise aspect of prayer has evolved out of an evocation practice, or perhaps even invocation. If this is so, then the measure of success in praise prayer has to be less to do with humouring the deity, and more to do with attuning and understanding.

From experience, the time when prayer has been least effective for me has been during periods of crisis. Creating a sense of peace and sacredness is much harder when starting from a place of turmoil, conflict or pain. I've found distress a real barrier to meaningful prayer work, and at the same time these circumstance create the greatest desire to able to petition and get results. Thus, in crisis, the inability of prayer to provide tangible results is more painfully evident than ever. The crisis itself may distract you from the sacred, leaving you to feel that you have been abandoned in the hour of your greatest need.

In times of crisis, the idea of deity as uber-parent, able to make the world a safe and agreeable place on demand, is something we can find ourselves wanting to believe in. There's nothing like a realisation of personal powerlessness to make a person want some external power source they can tap into. At that point, prayer may indeed be a reflection of our need for connection and our inability to survive alone.

When life is going smoothly, we tend not to think about it. We are more likely to see the easy periods as being the default, than to imagine divine influence smoothing the way for us. In times of trouble, we ask where god is and how "he" let this happen. People readily offer the Second World War as an example of the absence of god. If something had been prevented of course we would not be able to see it, which make this whole approach to thinking about deity and prayer seem a little bit pointless. We get what we get. Frequently it isn't what we thought we wanted. Sometimes it might turn out to be what we need. Often what matters most is what we choose to make of what we get. Failure or learning experience? Disaster or opportunity? We do not create reality by imagining it, but how we think about it informs what we are able to do with it.

The person who prays to have the problem taken away will tend to see little change. The person who prays for the means to keep going may more readily find their own power and strength. The person who prays for insight opens themselves to inspiration.

Like any other tool or process, prayer will work when used in the right ways, and fail utterly when used badly. If we use prayer to seek easy solutions, avoid challenges, get something for nothing, or avoid responsibility, then little good will come of it. Whether they are answered or unanswered, ultimately such prayers cannot help us.

The person who prays to cultivate inner qualities is in a very different position. That may be seen as an empowering dialogue with the self, needing no divine influence to be wholly effective as a psychological process. The person who prays for hope, opportunity and ways forward becomes open to seeing those things, again regardless of whether you believe in external influences. If the divine or spiritual intercedes, the person still has to work to resolve things, still learns, grows and holds responsibility. Praying for help can work in all kinds of ways. Praying to have it all done for you is of no use at all.

On a personal note, I came to writing this section after a short period of personal crisis. For a time, I felt utterly powerless and experienced longing for a deity who could offer me justice, protection and generally fix everything. That impulse remained strong, despite a personal belief that such prayers are futile. I found I could not pray at all, due to loss of inner calm and an inability to focus. Being unable to pray added to my feelings of isolation and despair.

I had a life experience which I approached with the belief that I needed it to work in my favour. I imagined that said experience could affirm my sense of self, help me overcome old pain and generally improve my life. When this all failed to happen, I had an initial experience of crushing defeat, pain and humiliation. My whole sense of self hung in the balance. Either I could internalise some damning feedback about myself, or I could choose something different. I could uphold all my greatest fears about my shortcomings, or I could consider the many positive reflections offered back by the people around me.

In a blinding moment of insight and inspiration, I realised that if I kept pinning my sense of self to things on the outside, I would always have these problems. If I did not accept myself as a viable and decent person, no external source could ever give me that.

I went back to prayer looking not for a magical solution, but for ways in which I could take my spiritual work forwards. This in turn enabled me to see where others in my life had acted unreasonably, and to understand how I could take positive action. Prayers for instant solutions, if answered, would not have given me the much-needed healing that eventually came. Out of pain and humiliation I forged a stronger identity. Is that a case of the gods sending me what I truly needed, or is it that I used the strength grown in spiritual work to turn a nightmare scenario into one of redemption?

I reflect that having offered myself as a tool for peace and harmony, I find myself placed in positions to take on those who abuse their power. Arguably, I have been given exactly what I prayed for. I have opportunities to increase overall peace and harmony by challenging those who act to harm and disquiet. I have found a solution to some of my petitioned-over problems, albeit at a considerable price. Is this evidence of prayers being answered, or just a natural unfolding of reality, unaffected by deity, prayer or intent? I cannot know. I have to embrace that uncertainty.

I go forwards conscious that prayer might have changed things for me. As a consequence, I will go back to whispering into the void at night.

Hello spirits of peace and harmony. Spirits of restorative justice, poetic justice and compassion. Show me how to work for you in the world. Show me where to push and how to speak. I want to make a difference. Teach me deeper compassion and the means to make justice and peace.

Chapter Five

The Ethics of Prayer

At first glance, prayer may seem like an unquestionably ethical practice. From a religious point of view, prayer may in fact be the essential attribute of the religious life. Still, I feel it is important to ask, is it always ethically sound to pray?

If you believe in a single, supreme and benevolent God, the answer tends towards a straightforward "yes". Assuming the existence of such a being postulates a reality in which your prayers are considered carefully by a deity who can see the bigger picture. The all-powerful good god is not going to answer evil prayers with action. We won't have much hope of understanding how such a being will judge what we ask for, and there's the whole issue of a grand plan into which we have no insight. Therefore prayers in this scenario can only be answered if they fit with the bigger picture. The supreme being chooses to give or withhold, while the petitioner holds no responsibility for the outcome. After all, what you asked for can only happen if the god thinks it was a good idea, too.

However, even in this setup, the individual is still responsible for everything they do and do not do. The person who prays rather than taking action has made a choice to which there will be an ethical dimension. Where behaviour is in any way shaped by prayer, then the role of prayer can be considered as an ethical issue. Furthermore, the person who cultivates habits of unethical thinking, even when appealing to a benevolent god, will affect their own psyche in unpleasant ways. Those who feed anger, envy and hatred will fill themselves with those emotions, and that in turn has consequences.

Prayer ethics are even more complex when we consider the implications of prayer in a polytheistic context. All the pantheons

I am aware of have their share of darker gods, or deities with darker aspects. Forces of war and vengeance, destruction, death and suffering. The diversity of nature is represented in Pagan pantheons, and nature is not inherently gentle. If I pray to fairly benevolent deities for passably reasonable things, this is very different from praying to personifications of rage to bring destruction on my enemies. In theory at least, I am involving powers with intentions of their own in order to try to get my way. Whatever the rights and wrongs of a given petition, I think the key point is this: if you hold a polytheistic view and pray to a specific god for a specific outcome, the ethics of what you do are entirely your responsibility.

This may not be as comfortable an arrangement as it first seems. For example, imagine that I am struggling to get much-needed empathy and compassion from a person who has power over me. I am not asking to have it all my own way here, just not to be pushing against an immovable object. I ask for intervention. The other person gets a learning experience so brutal that it tears their whole life apart, after which they are indeed a bit more sympathetic about my problems because they've just experienced something similar. I might carefully choose to view that as an interesting coincidence. I might interpret it as proof that I am beloved of the gods and that I have a lot of power. I may be overcome by guilt or remorse. As for the person who received the learning experience I explicitly prayed for, can I say if they are better or worse off now, or what the rights and wrongs of it are? Each outcome we might get in a given situation has its own consequences, and rare is a situation simply good or bad, even from the most subjective viewpoint. Be careful what you pray for. An apparently answered prayer may be much more disturbing than the uncomplicated silence.

Atheist perspectives raise numerous criticisms of prayer, with an eye to the ethical implications. The most common complaint stems from a fear that prayer will be used as an alternative to practical action. Where prayer is a sane kind of private self-help activity, atheists tend not to be so critical, but examples like parents refusing medical help for children in favour of relying on a god is likely to evoke anger. Understandably so. Blind faith in the infallibility of anything is dangerous.

When you start by assuming that nothing exists which can respond to prayers, what we do in prayer becomes a purely human consideration. The modern perspective (post-industrialisation) that equates worldly success with divine favour would be a prime example of this in action. If you are able to have your own way and enjoy material success, it is easy to think that your prayers apparently being answered is proof of divine favour. Therefore, being in power, having resources, and success demonstrates your spiritual excellence. Poverty is, from this perspective, proof of vice and unholiness. Therefore those who are manifestly beloved of God need do nothing for those whose lack of effort and spirituality has been their downfall. By this means, unfair systems and abuses can be justified by people who choose to feel good about their tyranny and privilege.

If you win a war and see divine favour in this, then the justification for inflicting atrocities on the loser is right there. There is no honour in any of this. The more we imagine gods as being present and active in the world, the more easily we may distort interpretations of worldly success into proof of divine favour. Beliefs about karma and reincarnation can be used in the same way, with misfortune ascribed to past life misdemeanours, relieving the more fortunate from feeling any need to share their good fortune.

My feeling is that the person who wants justifications for the status quo, for their own good luck or inaction, will find that somewhere. Taking away the idea of prayer and divine favour will not change this aspect of human behaviour. Evolution, innate superiority of class, gender, race, bloodline, etc. can all be wheeled out to the same unpleasant effect. It is also true that the person intent on the spiritual life, wishing to live honourably and feeling compassion for those less fortunate than themselves, will do the best they can regardless of whether prayer is a part of their lives.

Implications of Belief

For the next section of this chapter, I'm going to consider prayer with the assumption that it does work, including the idea that petition can be assumed capable of creating change. I'm doing this not as a statement of faith in prayer as the source of supernatural intervention, but to explore the implications of that belief. This is to allow me to consider the impact of this approach without getting bogged down in caveats at every turn. I still hold my uncertainty, but, for the purposes of argument, how do the ethics of prayer need considering if you can get what you ask for?

Is it ethical to pray for someone else? If the person you have in mind belongs to the same faith as you and feels positive about the idea of prayer then clearly there's less issue. Christians can probably assume that other Christians will be fine about being prayed for. But, what if you are praying for them to get over being gay so that they can come back into the fold? What if your prayers are for changes and "improvements" the other person doesn't want?

I've had Christians tell me they would pray for my soul so that I would see the light and get free of all this nasty Pagan stuff. It wasn't a helpful experience and evidently did not change me, but it did entirely compromise a relationship.

All-knowing gods can probably be trusted to sort these things out for us. However, if the gods are not all-knowing, they do not necessarily know what the best outcome would be, either. It is to be hoped they have a better idea than we do, or some perspective, but it depends so much on who you appeal to and how they relate to your circumstances. Angry gods are not going to do much to teach you patience or tolerance, even if that is what you most need right now.

I feel uncomfortable praying for people in anything but the broadest terms. If I want to help someone, I'll ask that they find what they need. If I'm struggling in conflict with someone, I try to ask that they get helpful learning experiences and insight, rather than boils, but as previously observed, that's not without issue.

The only way to know if people outside your faith group feel comfortable being prayed for, is to ask. My current rule of thumb is that if I wouldn't feel comfortable asking, it's a non-starter. If people are asking for prayers and positive thoughts, that's an open invitation and I'll do what I can. When thinking about other people I'm mostly inclined to go for a "dear universe" approach to praying anyway. I do not feel that I have a divine sanction to interfere in other people's lives by praying to specific deities for specific outcomes.

Dear universe, my friend here is having a hard time and could do with a couple of days to get over the last round of crap you delivered. A breathing space in which nothing difficult happens would be really welcome just now. Thank you.

One of the consequences of praying for people is to feel that no further action is then required. It can also result in us feeling better in the face of tragedy or disaster. In *Benevolent Magic & Living Prayer* Robert Shapiro says with regard to such scenarios, "It will help you to feel better because you are doing something."[17] And, "You won't feel frustrated"[18] the media floods our lives with awareness of suffering across the globe. Taking this on-board is almost impossible, and trying to hold compassion for all those in pain out there is beyond most of us, and certainly beyond me. Responding to crisis with prayer can give us the feeling we are doing something useful, and this in turn eases our discomfort. Is that a good thing? Perhaps sometimes it is.

It is vitally important that prayer does not replace direct action. If we allow prayer to feed a sense of self-importance...*I've prayed for you, that's enough, God listens to me...* we court not only ethical issues, but also psychological problems. The person who starts to believe their prayers alone can change the world, will end up wholly detached from reality. No matter how seriously you take your prayer work, it is essential to hold doubt and uncertainty too. For the sake of maintaining good mental health, some scepticism is needed. If you pray for something, and it happens, the other possible reasons for that outcome need to stay with you. After all, if it did work, the power behind the change came from somewhere. That's wholly different from spell work and from practical action, and needs thinking about carefully.

Getting into the habit of praying for others can help us engage with the world. Prayer can be used to strengthen resolve and develop awareness as we look out for those who need help. Prayer can reinforce practical action rather than replace it. We can seek strength and integrity through prayer to support practical action.

There have been times in my life when, in fear and rage, my thoughts about other people have been destructive. When no real-world justice is forthcoming, when someone threatens your hearth, home, family, livelihood, neighbourhood, culture, community... When you are powerless in face of danger or outrage, ill wishing is a natural enough response. That desire to have the otherwise unassailable source of our woes struck by lightning or eaten by bears, or for their evil machinations to backfire in some way that brings poetic justice. If the recorded curses listed in *The Magical Universe*[19] are at all indicative, we've been petitioning to have our enemies laid low for quite some time.

Having the wrath of gods blow up our hate figures, might be both satisfying and validating, as well as solving a few problems. Many an act of violence has been justified by this kind of logic.

That it is tempting, widespread and natural does not make ill-wishing ethical. We might consider, as Melusine Draco does in *By Spellbook and Candle*,[20] the ethics of redressing power imbalances, righting wrongs where no other justice is available, and so forth. My feeling on this score is that if I wouldn't do it in person, I shouldn't do it by occult or spiritual means either. I do pray for poetic justice, though.

I've had considerable opportunity to explore my own anger and the effects of my own negative thinking. Feeling both anger and powerlessness makes ill-wishing and malevolent prayer appealing. I imagine that if this resulted in discernible effects, the person praying for retribution might feel satisfied. This is a guess because my fury has yet to result in any pianos falling from the sky. What I have observed is the way in which angry prayer seemed to reinforce my feelings of frustration and powerlessness. I ascribe this to the influence of time spent holding extremely negative thoughts.

Once I changed my thinking (not just prayer, but my whole attitude) towards a more positive outlook; seeking peace, freedom and harmony, my mood improved and I felt better within myself. I see this as a largely psychological effect.

We are the sum of our thoughts, feelings and actions. Time spent on angry, vengeful petitions to the universe is time spent reinforcing things we may wish to be free from. The effects we have upon our own minds and souls should be part of our consideration while pondering the ethics of prayer.

However, if we pray for strength and the ability to tolerate, seeking compassion for others and kindness to them, there can be unsought consequences. Praying for the strength to carry on may help to hold a victim in an abusive relationship, be that at home or at work. Asking that we be gentler, more tolerant people is good in many contexts, but if we are being bullied and used, such an approach will only help to keep us on our knees. If prayer is to be ethical, then compassion for self and compassion for others must be held in a healthy balance.

Islam postulates prayer as seeking submission to the will of Allah. Some Christian writers will also talk about putting yourself entirely in God's hands. From this readily comes the understanding that everything we experience is the will of deity, and, if we are too sure of ourselves, that everything we do is also God's will. This can lead to chronic hubris, twisted logic and acts of cruelty. As observed before, I hold this to be the responsibility of the individual, not deity. Telling ourselves that we have submitted to the will of gods is not the same as doing it. The person who wants excuses will find them, here or somewhere else. When the idea of getting everyone to submit to the will of a god, or the gods, is in vogue with a religion or culture, the results are vicious. Once we start to believe that we have submitted, know what the gods want and are therefore both able and obliged to make other people do things, for their own good, we are in a lot of trouble. The person who truly seeks the divine will rapidly realise that you can't meaningfully force religion on others. Submission only works when it comes from within. If forced onto a person, religion becomes abuse. Any attempt at using a religious practice to hold authority, is a failure of spirituality.

A person who prays to submit to the will of a god, or the gods, may go through life able to stoically accept what comes to them. They may develop inner peace, acceptance or the ability to see a silver lining in every cloud. Equally, such a person could become complacent or apathetic, or respond with passive submissiveness to things it might be better to resist. We could contemplate all forms of martyrdom in this light. It is also worth considering how humanly subjective the idea of "better" is and whether anyone should be entitled to force their understanding of "better" on to someone else. My notion of "better", for example, includes small living spaces and not owning much, which many people would not find comfortable.

Some books about prayer encourage readers to pray for anything and everything where ease is desired. This tends to be more of a trait of New Age writing, where a self-centred world view is often encouraged. What happens when we pray about everything? This would depend in part on the nature of the prayers, and what they were supposed to achieve. Many religions and religious thinkers take the approach of using prayer to ask the divine to be with a person through the day, and present to people in mundane things. This can have the effect of making all things seem more inherently sacred, and developing awareness that anything can be done in a spiritual way. Most religions are not constructed around an objective to provide brief weekly social contact, but are meant to be fully present in our lives. Approaching prayer in this way, a person might ask their ancestors to help them act responsibly. They may seek to take Jesus with them so that their shopping choices are as ethical as possible. A Buddhist may be praying for the inner calm needed to uphold Buddhist principles in the workplace. A Pagan might ask the spirits of place to guide them towards seeing how to hold balance, and so forth. This is all about holding an innately spiritual attitude and taking our values with us into whatever we are doing. There is nothing unethical here.

Much mainstream culture encourages competition, selfishness and greed. It is often helpful to have a support mechanism – of which prayer is an example – if you are trying to step away from all of that. Using prayer to construct and maintain inner states that allow you to uphold spiritual values in normal life, can be part of being a religious or spiritual person. Obviously the values you are trying to uphold need considering on their individual merits, but the method is solid enough and will not automatically create unethical behaviour.

What happens when we pray over everything, not to bring spirituality into our lives, but as a quick fix? Robert Shapiro suggests, for example, that we pray to easily find a parking space when going to get a haircut.[21] Firstly, I think that trivial prayer can encourage the mind-set that everything should, ideally, be easy for us. A life free from challenge is also largely devoid of opportunities to grow and learn. Humans thrive on challenges and often it is difficulty that reveals to us the very best in our own natures. It is nigh on impossible to experience many virtues – courage, integrity, creativity, steadfastness, loyalty, determination, and resilience for example – without there being some kind of challenge to bring them out. In many ways, prayers requesting that life be made easy are prayers requesting that we are not required to change or make much effort. It's just as well that this kind of petition seldom works.

Focusing prayer on trivial issues of personal "need", when we mistake minor wants for necessities, has other direct consequences too. We reinforce to ourselves the idea that these trivial wants are actually important needs. The parking problems of an affluent western lifestyle are a product of an excessively easy lifestyle in the first place. The more importance we give to trivia like this, the less time we have for the larger and more troubling issues of the world, and for the important issues of our own lives. What does it mean to be praying for a parking space when there are wars, famines, injustices and extinctions? This kind of prayer practice will encourage us to focus on the self, and overestimate the significance of our own problems, whilst turning spirituality into yet another consumer service.

Dear God, I'd like a faster car, a new carpet for the living room, those shoes to be in the sale next week, and a parking space. I don't want to work for these things and I hold them to be more important and worthy of your attention right now than world peace or starving children.

A brief consideration of right wing "Christian" politics in America would suggest plenty of people do think and pray in this way. As I remember it though, "Greed is good" was a line from a contemporary film, not a spiritual text.

If you struggle with the daily challenges, it makes more sense to focus prayer on the need for developing qualities within yourself. Rather than pray for the parking space, pray to have greater patience. Simply by focusing on the quality you want to develop, you strengthen it within yourself. Even without divine intervention, this kind of prayer works in the same way that any positive thinking technique will. It supports, develops and encourages more productive ways of thinking, which doesn't raise much in the way of ethical difficulty.

Getting the magical parking space is unlikely to change your life. If you are a grumpy, impatient kind of person it probably won't even improve your day by much. If the prayer towards cultivating patience has any effect, it will be far further reaching.

A great deal of human behaviour comes down to habits of both thought and action. Prayer gives us a space in which we can imagine a more ideal self and work towards inner change. Much of our life experience can be changed by shifting how we think about it. Even more can be changed by learning to control or alter our reactions. Just the shift from reacting automatically to considering what we might do has considerable impact. Finally, if we work to develop the inner qualities we need, we are better able to act meaningfully in the world. If we want to act ethically, we need to develop the means for that within ourselves. We can't pray to be ethical and expect that to work all by itself. We can pray to be ethical as part of a process in which we use prayer to try and do the right things for the right reasons, and with our actions supporting that work.

The person who prays for a parking space is not poised to change. The person who prays for and discovers patience may learn to be gentler with themselves, undertaking not to try to cram in so much that they have to rush all the time. Perhaps they decide to leave the car behind and walk to the appointment, liberated from the need to find a parking space at all.

We always have the right to change ourselves. Prayer that

focuses on inner change tends to be more ethically nurturing than prayer that seeks easy external solutions. There remains the risk of too much self-absorption, though. Balance is the key to all virtues, to health, sustainability and a workable system of personal ethics. Time spent looking inwards is good and necessary. Too much time spent looking inwards leads to self-obsession, loss of perspective and courts disconnection from wider reality. Balance between the inner and outer life is essential.

That issue of becoming disconnected from the rest of the world is the final destination for this chapter. Much of the prayer work suggested by religious thinkers, regardless of tradition, has nothing to do with petition. Prayer is more about entering into a relationship with the divine, being open to the voice of spirit; open to direction and inspiration. Prayer is an invitation to the numinous to enter your life. When none of this actually happens, prayer is an act of ritual, affirming belief and a sense of belonging. The practitioner who puts in ten minutes a day may feel psychological benefits and suffer no ills.

The trouble starts if prayer works. Imagine being lifted out of your mundane life into a moment of rapture; bathed in love, overwhelmed with a sense of worth and belonging. For a tiny moment, all is beauty and wonder. There is a feeling that everything makes sense, has a point and is not just there to torment you until you die. Imagine a keen sense that there is some great spiritual force out there and that, right now, its love and benevolence are shining upon you.

The moment passes and the numinous light fades away. You are back in a cold, hostile and uncertain world where pain and challenges are a given. Of course you want to go back. You want more. Perhaps you want this all the time. The numinous can be addictive. I have had a few, tantalising flashes. They made everything else I was doing at the time seem less important to me than they would otherwise have been. When that enormity seems real to me, when I hold that sense of the numinous, all I want to do is follow it. I want to stay in that space. Rationally, I know I can't and that I need the "out there" perspective to give meaning to what happens "in here". But it is like a drug, or it can be.

I used to be confused by the weird things historical mystics got up to: sitting at the top of poles in the desert; taking up hermit residence in distant caves; being bricked into the corner of a church. For a long time I saw this as a kind of spiritual masochism and a bit crazy. In this last year or so, my perspective has shifted. The desire to give up all worldly things in pursuit of the numinous now makes sense to me. There have been plenty of days when I could have disappeared off into a cave, eschewing all things bodily in the hopes of achieving one more glimpse.

In many ways, this is also what happens to a lot of drug addicts. Think of the folk who end up homeless, living from one fix to the next, their life consumed by the rapture. What I have between my ears is all brain chemistry. Recreational drugs can only work by tapping in to existing potential. This is not to reduce spiritual experience to the level of an internally generated body chemistry acid trip. However, it might pay us to think carefully about what happens inside us when we are having a spiritual experience.

I hit a point where my philosophy and experience started to diverge. My Druidry is very much about being present in the world. Experience of prayer, however, started to take me out of the world. I wanted to be in that other place so much that the spiritual dimensions of the rest of life became less important. Then, as inexplicably as the door opened, it closed again. The numinous experiences went away and I had to step back and seriously reconsider what I was doing, and why.

Since then, I've experienced cycles of awareness and unawareness that seem to depend on a number of factors. The frequency with which I give time to prayer is critical and I find that the more I do, the easier it becomes to achieve a sense of the numinous. The more oppressed I am by depression, anxiety and other negative emotional states, the less able I am able to feel a sense of connection. However, it is these diminished moods that are most likely to induce a desire to pray in the first place. It has been my experience so far that prayer is most uplifting when nothing in particular is sought, while praying for solutions to problems only reinforces my despondency.

What I pray for also dramatically impacts on my experience. If I pray for any kind of intervention, I actually increase my feelings of powerlessness and so end up feeling more demoralised and overwhelmed. My sense that everything is beyond my control can be increased by this kind of prayer. However, if I consider the qualities I need to draw on within myself, and pray that those be reinforced, I am strengthening that which I need, regardless of any deity involvement. If I pray for courage, strength or resilience, for example, I reinforce my sense of having the necessary qualities to draw on.

This has led me to consider the way in which formal religion encourages us to pray. So much formal prayer seems to place power and responsibility in the hands of deity, not the individual. If my sample population of one is a fair example, this has sinister implications: the more a religion encourages you to pray for help, the more disempowered and demoralised you may become. This needs the kind of psychological research that uses decent numbers of test subjects and is wholly beyond me. Still, I think it worth watching for. The New Age tendency to pray for everything to be made easier may actually have the effect of making life harder and more painful.

When we think about prayer, the ethical impact of the experience of praying as it affects the psychology of the individual, is of tremendous importance. We must consider what we do to ourselves, what others ask of us, and what we in turn do to others if we invite them to pray.

Chapter Six

Standing Before the Unknown

Doubt is fundamental to the human condition. We may have faith in deities, but we can never hope to know what (if anything) deity really is. If deity exists as something outside of us, then by definition it goes beyond anything we can comprehend. The whole point of gods seems to be that they know and understand more than we do and are able to do things we cannot. Any kind of rational approach to spirituality calls for a bit of doubt – in our own ability to understand, in the available sum of human knowledge that might guide us, in the meaning and source of our experience, and so forth. It is doubt, not faith, which forms the basis of more viable and compassionate approaches to religion. Too much belief without evidence leads to fundamentalism, which in turn begets hatred and inflexibility. It is better, I think, not to put your faith in gods, but to carry your doubt towards the possibility of them, and see what happens.

Doubt does not in any way exclude the possibility of belief. We can believe whatever we like. Alongside that, holding our doubt, we are also alert to the limits of our insight. With doubt, we recognise that there could always be other ways of understanding things. This in turn allows us to see other people's beliefs as equally valid.

It seems deeply irrational to me to imagine that, as a human, I could hope to understand how spirit, mystery, or deity function. I've read books that purport to hold all the answers, and these seem to engage my capacity for disbelief far more readily than anything else does. The more certain a person is about ultimate truths, the less plausible I find them. As a consequence, when I come to prayer, I am always approaching the unknown with no expectations about what might happen. This feeling of uncertainty heightens my sense of wonder and my appreciation of the numinous. These experiences do not fit neatly into human definitions. When we try to control our experiences to make them fit a pre-imagined shape, we may miss the more ephemeral aspects that had the most to teach us.

I have no desire for coherence. I do not want neat or tidy answers to life, the universe, and everything; that would reduce the enormity of life, death and being in ways I do not find attractive. While I do not find scientific explanations in any way diminish my experience of the material world, I do not want spirit to be so tidy. On an emotional level, I crave mystery and enjoy not knowing. I have a keen sense there are things that, as a human, it is none of my business to know anyway. Having no personal experience of absolute religious certainty to refer to, I have no direct insight into what it means to pray because you think God wants you to. I assume that kind of certainty can only be held if your story includes an explanation for why prayer does not work.

Early on in my prayer work, before my efforts had any discernible effect, I started to consider the implications of what I had undertaken. Coming from a place of no definite faith in deity, I was trying to attract the attention of some kind of vast, powerful entity. I don't do blind faith and I don't undertake religious activity for the sake of it, generally. Up until this point in my life, I had sought experience above all else. Did I want the attention of divine beings? The idea frightened me. Did I want to hear voices? Our culture pathologises what in the past would have counted as religious experience. Is it the case that all religious experience is simply the consequence of failed mental health? Was I willing to gamble with my sanity over this? I had to consider what might happen to me if I did start hearing voices. I felt fear. So much fear that I seriously considered going no further. After a while, curiosity won out over anxiety. The desire to know something, to experience, proved stronger than the fear of consequences.

For the person who sees the universe as inherently benevolent, the idea of encountering the divine may seem less alarming. Even then, the enormity of the prospect could well intimidate and perhaps, should. There is a fine line between awe and awful, between wonder and terror. That which overwhelms is almost bound to startle, if not shock. Trying to turn the idea of divinity into something tame, safe and predictable, seems pointless to me. Such an approach is all about trying to project our desires onto life, rather than exploring what is actually out there.

There's nothing like trying to encounter the divine to make you realise just how small and finite you are. So there you are, in the position and location of your choice, poised to go "Um… hello?" At this point, the usefulness of a formal prayer tradition becomes a good deal more apparent. Having a set bunch of things to say, already tried and tested, is enormously comforting but means you don't have to think so much about the process. What do you actually want to say to the divine? It is also worth contemplating what you would like the divine to say to you. If anything. Consider what it would be like if the divine undertook to say anything at all. By this I do not mean some experience you suspect yourself of having imagined or intuited. Complete, direct, unmistakable communication is the concept to contemplate here. What would that mean?

Thus far I've not had that kind of direct, verbal response. It is about as much as I can cope with to have a sense that something might possibly be out there listening. While, with practise, I have found it easier to experience a sense of the divine, I find it incredibly hard to stay there. I want to stay there, but holding my mind in a state of receptiveness is not easy. Repeatedly finding this to be the case, I started to rethink the whole idea of petition. Having a list of things you want to say – be that petitioning, expressions of gratitude, or traditional prayers you can repeat, can keep the mind in place. It's also a good deal less intimidating. The rich, golden silence of the numinous is something I find hard to bear for long periods, no matter how much I want it.

If I take my words into that space, it feels a bit less insane. With my words I also bring a few helpful limitations and a bit of humanity. This, in turn, probably does restrict my direct experience, but I have come to appreciate that this is a good thing. There is only so much I can take, and it looks like my mind is quite capable of protecting me from madness by losing focus before things get out of control.

I imagine that for this kind of work, the soft flow of a mantra or rosary would be ideal. I've not found anything Pagan that would function for me in the same way, nor have I managed to write anything suitable.

One of the recurring themes in books about prayer from many traditions, is the idea of making the self open to, and available to, the divine. Most formal religions take a person towards submission to deity. Very few Pagans of my acquaintance have seemed interested in this kind of process. Most Druids consider relationship an intrinsic part of Druidry. We may not seek opportunities to submit to anything. The quest for relationship, and the deepening of relationship, is very much the work of a Druid. This means that being open to deity makes a lot of sense in Druidry, but total submission doesn't.

I've commented before that we need not limit ourselves to praying to the divine. In theory, it is possible to approach anything, or anyone, through the medium of prayer. I don't think that coming to the known with prayer lacks scope for a sense of mystery and wonder.

For example, let us imagine that we approach the spirit of a place in a prayerful way. At first we might contemplate the physical reality of the place, the way sunlight falls upon it, and the shape of the ground. Even in the smallest grove, the quantity and diversity of life is amazing. Each living thing is unique, a small miracle in its own right. Even without belief in anything outside nature, we can experience awe in a prayer to that which is around us.

In many ways, prayer is an attempt at a conversation, but will probably turn out to be a monologue. However, regardless of what comes back to us, the attempt itself raises awareness of that which is not us. By engaging creatively and imaginatively, by trying to connect, we will change ourselves a bit. It may be that deep contemplation will prove more effective if you tend towards an atheist view, but there's a fine line between this and prayer.

As Druids, we also have the option of praying to the awen. As is so often the case, whether this makes sense will depend a lot on what, exactly, you believe. Praying to the flow of inspiration can be a way of trying to draw it into your life. The quest for inspiration is so central to Druid life and in many ways is a great mystery as well. What is the awen? Where does it come from and how does it flow to us? Where does it flow from? The mystery of the process of inspiration underpins the wonderful book, *Zen and the Art of Motorcycle Maintenance,* which I recommend reading if this subject appeals to you. Elusive and precious, the mechanism of inspiration remains unknown. We cannot pin down how it works. Even if we saw it as an event in the brain, captured in flashing lights and moving dials, we'd still need to know what happened just before then to make it possible, and just before that. Sometimes connections form in the mind in an instant, and there seems to be no reason for it all to come together. The brain itself is a great mystery and source of wonder. We are not likely to unpick the physical mechanics of inspiration in a way that will allow us to possess it, and yet so much human activity depends on that unexpected flash of inspiration.

In opening ourselves to mystery, we can also be more open to inspiration and it may be appropriate to consider the two as largely the same thing. New ideas might be understood as coming to us from the unknown. We make momentary bridges between ourselves and the rest of existence. Something is understood. Inspiration flows.

I'm tempted to see the awen as the purest, most essential kind of inspiration. It is the inspiration that comes to make life better, richer and more beautiful. Sacred inspiration is not the means to cheat or dominate others. It does not exist to give us the fast, irresponsible buck. To use the awen dishonourably is to betray it, so perhaps one of the things we might go to in prayer is the quest for insight as to how best to use what we find in our lives.

In bardic initiations, we swear to use our inspiration for the good of the land and tribe. In many ways, this dedication also functions as a prayer to the bardic tradition itself, that it holds us and keeps us on the right path.

Anything can be prayed to and, in praying, we catch glimpses of the mysteries that lie beneath the surface world we inhabit. Pray to the bardic tradition and you may encounter the wonder of a way of life that spans centuries, with its call to service and beauty. So many lives have been given to bardic work, so many voices creating a living tradition and a rich history we can draw on. Marvel at how the words of our ancestors are still available to us! Old stories come to life at the retelling. We can dance to tunes that inspired other feet, hundreds of years ago. Here too is mystery. Here is power and awe.

After a while exploring this it can start to feel as though this physical realm we inhabit is nothing but a thin veneer disguising an infinity of mysteries. Dare to contemplate the structure of an atom or the distance between stars. Dare to look into the eyes of another living being and see their absolute separateness and individuality. From inside that other, unknowable mind, a whole other universe exists, shaped around that individual perception, just as you are the centre of your own reality. How can we speak to each other across such incredible distances of awareness and understanding? And yet, we do.

What happens if we continue off down that line of thought? I came, I think inevitably, to the idea that all forms of communication could be approached as though they were sacred acts of prayer. I see the mystery in you. I see the spirit and the wonder. I honour that, and therefore to speak to you is to open the most sacred of dialogues. I pray to you and, just as I would when approaching other spirits, I must be willing to listen in respectful silence to hear your answer. In the messy haste of careless human interaction, this is not terribly viable much of the time.

Just as with approaching deity, if I tried to act in that way all the time, I'd go rapidly round the bend. The human mind has limits, and the realities of life place requirements on us all. Most of the people I know would be disturbed and upset if I tried to approach them in a prayerful way. It would not be conducive to buying potatoes, especially if I took the time to recognise the sacred life force of the potato and to pray for its acceptance of my taking it home and eating it.

There are needful balances to strike. There are times to contemplate the mystery, and offer up prayer. And times when socks need to be washed. There are times when sitting soulfully, conscious of the spirit within the person who sits beside you, is a beautiful way to be. There are times when the other person just wants to buy a bar of soap and leave. As I've said before, to be a Druid is to be present in the world. Part of what is called for in the quest to experience mystery, is the good sense to know when not to be doing that. Sometimes what matters most is the simple, immediate experience of life in the moment.

The shorter a period of time you intend to spend standing before the unknown, the easier it is. The less risk you have of anything happening, for a start. This makes the whole process less threatening. The prayers offered by religions tend to be short enough for easy learning. *Grant, oh spirits, thy protection...give us this day our daily bread... there is no God but Allah...* The length of most prayers is such that if we come to them from a normal, mundane headspace, at best by the end of the prayer we might be slightly open. All that time, we were doing the talking, it is worth noting. Do we think the gods are listening to barely considered repetitions of old formulae? Do we imagine anything out there really cares?

The function of this kind of prayer is not to help us achieve awareness. It is about showing up and expressing some sort of intent. That could lead somewhere. If you do this, you are a person who prays and it might be an important part of your life and identity, even if it brings nothing else. If you go through the motions, with no real care or attention, nothing is going to happen. It doesn't matter whether you define spirituality in terms of psychology or deity, put little in and the results will be minimal.

First and foremost, to stand before the unknown is to recognise the existence of the unknown. That which is bigger than we are. That which transcends our understanding. Prayer is an act of opening awareness that puts our small lives into important perspective. Most of the time we need to protect these fragile, human minds by not letting them be swamped with how much there is outside of us. We tune out far more sensory information than we allow into our conscious awareness. However, it benefits us to drop that defence now and then, to consider the terrifying, glorious enormity of it all. Death. Infinity. Eternity. You might call it deity, you might not. Of course our human natures want the enormity to wear a friendly face, pat us gently on the head and say, "Well done, keep up the good work." Of course we want mystery to be on a manageable, human scale. This is why we like to give bits of it names, beards, clothing preferences and stories. Religion is all about making the unimaginable possible to engage with. Prayer is all about letting go of those stories again to try to encounter what we cannot hope to comprehend.

I cannot tell you what it means to stand in that place of awareness for a few seemingly bright seconds. I'd love to say it's like this familiar thing, or that other thing you do, and bring it down to a more mundane level. If I did that, I wouldn't be telling you what it is like. We go there for ourselves, or not at all.

I'm conscious that I am barely skimming the surface of mystery and that many others will have gone far deeper in their quests. I have only deliberately worked with prayer for about a year now. I have an advantage in that nearly two decades' worth of meditation work have given me some mental discipline and I know how to open my mind a bit. I can be still and quiet. It also helps that I can shift fairly easily from dealing with the mundane, to states of mind appropriate for ritual and trance. I find those same sorts of mental states are necessary for prayer.

What I struggle to do, is to remain in that place of openness to mystery for more than very short bursts. My psyche simply cannot maintain it, and I recognise there may be very good reasons not to go too far, anyway. Practice is no doubt key here, returning over and over to a deliberate opening up, and listening, to glimpse some fleeting thing and fall away again. It feels very much as though I am breaking my mind open. Perhaps if I managed to do this all at once, my reason would not survive the experience. I am here to live in this world, not to gaze continuously at something else. It is absolutely essential therefore that I crack myself open gently, slowly and with care. Not just to avoid madness, but because I think there are other processes happening here and I suspect time is needed for those.

Life, death, time and infinity do not just exist inside my head. They are part of the world. Everything I might pray to is around me, all of the time. The atoms that made dinosaurs may be in the parsnip I eat for tea. Everything that happened in this material world still exists, even if it has taken a new shape. Everything is here and now. Time spent inside my head, in prayer, enables me to come out and glimpse things with my eyes open, too. Everything is here, and I am part of everything. This has taken me towards the insanities of knowing about the real world.

Contemplating the space between atoms and how, exactly, all of my atoms have been persuaded to travel around together. What is my consciousness, and why is it? The inside of my head turns out to be as enormous and inexplicable as the distances between stars. Thinking about any of it for too long makes my head ache. But, less of that happens than it used to. Day by day, prayer by prayer, I find myself a little bit more able to think about the vastness of everything and the possible implications. Each specific moment and manifestation of The Everything becomes that bit more clear and precious, as an individual, and also that bit more clearly a part of the unthinkable whole.

There is only so much time in a day that it is wise and productive to spend on this kind of work. Family must be fed, wood cut and clothes laundered. If The Everything takes over so that we no longer engage with individual manifestations, we are lost. Thus it is important to move slowly, to remain thoroughly grounded in the mundane realities of living. Touch the infinite softly and not too often. Let it open your eyes a little, but do not seek to know all at once. There isn't enough room inside a human mind for The Everything. That's rather the point.

Without that sliver of awareness of a bigger picture, we live without context. We forget that the way we treat the current forms in which The Everything is assembled, affects the future. We forget that all of time and existence created the moment we inhabit. If all we do is see the individualised surface; this tree, that person, my car, my holiday home, my private jet, my secluded island paradise... we forget the whole. Awareness of the whole reminds us of the part we play, the duty of care we have, the shared commons of air and water, the ridiculousness of imagining we own anything. The more time we give to the enormities, the better we are able to discriminate between mountains and molehills. Seeing a bigger picture is a great teacher, encouraging us to look past the minor irritations and victories of the moment to consider larger stories and more enduring needs.

As humans, we tend towards a destructive kind of arrogance. We can view everything from the ground beneath our feet to fellow human creatures as resources to use for our own gratification. Time spent seeking mysteries and attempting to stand before the unknown, challenges the user mindset. It is a little like inventing for yourself the machine Douglas Adams imagined in *The Hitchhiker's Guide to the Galaxy* that shows you the universe with you absent from it. It is important to be reminded of how tiny and insignificant we really are, and to break down our foolish assumptions of entitlement. We are no bigger than any other comparable cluster of atoms. No more or less important. We are stardust. We are the reincarnation of the first living proteins in the primordial swamps. We are dinosaur poo and the entrails of our ancestors. You may have some former Elvis atoms. I'd like to think that tiny bits of me once contributed to a giant, hairy cow. The raw material of the universe connects us. Stand before enormity, try to reach for The Everything, and you cannot escape the suggestion that we are part of that, and that it means something.

I feel such an absolute novice. There is nothing like a faint whiff or whisper of the numinous to make all striving and study feel like wobbly baby steps. The sheer enormity of all that I do not know and understand, grounds me, motivates me and fills me with awe. I have read a lot in the process of studying prayer, much of it written by people far older and wiser than myself. They do not have answers either. There are tested methods and words of encouragement; a sense that it is important and meaningful to pray even if you can't put those meanings into words. I have seen reflections of my own questioning in the words of others, but found little by way of answers.

Even authors who claim considerable authority and insight fail to explain what prayer is and does once it goes beyond a certain point. At first, this frustrated me. I had come to the subject full of intellectual interest, wanting academically framed answers. I found none. It would be easy to attribute that absence to the lack of inherent rationality and effectiveness in prayer and belief alike. Perhaps it cannot be explained because nothing actually happens. However, with so many people claiming that prayer does something for them, I could not entirely reject the process. Perhaps what prayer does is purely psychological. Does that matter? Placebos work. All of my life experience comes down to what I make of it, inside my head. A psychological event is no less real than a physical one to the person experiencing it.

I find that the uncertainty around the mechanics and realities of prayer does not detract from my sense of awe. Rather the opposite. Here I am, existing, unable to comprehend the functioning of my own mind. Are my spiritual experiences nothing more than self-induced events in my brain chemistry? That would be amazing, if it is a state of being we can trigger in ourselves at will! Is the idea of divinity a human construct, with no bearing on reality? How fabulous, if we, as a species have built and kept faith with such powerful concepts! If that is the size of it, then the human mind alone should be enough to fill us with awe and wonder.

And perhaps, in the vast, unknowable reaches of the universe, some sympathetic consciousness, or perhaps many such aware-nesses, are listening and trying to answer. Perhaps the rest of the universe is trying to talk to us all the time, and we have forgotten, or not yet learned how to hear.

I do not have answers, only a kind of cerebral, drunken enthusiasm for the questions. I cannot know. I want to know. It takes me back, over and over to sit in quiet darkness, trying to listen and wanting to understand. At the time of writing this in the original draft for this book, I am no longer saying "Hello" nor am I seeking help. I want to know how to be part of the solution. I want to know where I am needed and what my work should be. *If there are spirits of peace and harmony, please guide me. Point me at the jobs that need doing. Give me opportunity to contribute. I want to enable peace, justice and the flourishing of others.*

There have been no words or visions, no clarity, nor a definite message. In asking, I get better at listening – not just inside the headspace of prayer, but all the time. I'm listening to the people around me. To the news, to the physical realm which I inhabit. If someone comes to me, that is, really speaking, the universe speaking to me. A tiny fragment of the universe. We are all connected.

Day by day it becomes clearer to me that I am not looking for something just for myself in all of this. I want spaces in which I can work well. I'm aware of changing, and some of what shifts in me is the habit of prayer. Coming to understand that even if I could reliably petition for outcomes in my favour, the vast majority of the time I wouldn't want to. I want to live my life as well as I can and succeed on my own terms. If things are too easy, I do not find them so meaningful, although I am working on being more grateful for ease. "The more time I give to prayer, the less it sounds like, *"Please make this stuff go away"* and the more it comes out as, *"Bring it to me so that I can help"*.

Of course there is no saying how much of this shift is due to other life changes. My life may be an on-going experiment in being a Druid, but these are not laboratory conditions and the outcomes are not proof of anything. Is my life changing because I am praying, or am I praying because my life is changing? In this also, there is nothing to do but recognise the element of unknowableness, and carry on.

Chapter Seven

The Social Functions of Prayer

Thus far I have largely focused on the ways in which prayer might impact on the individual. However, that is only part of the story. Prayer can often be communal, and following prayer traditions also links us to others. When this is the case, there are social implications to praying. Prayer texts tend to be manifestations of formal religious traditions, raising considerations of the relationship between individual and tradition, as well. We can also consider prayer as a reflection of the individual's wider culture. Cause and effect move in all directions.

Picture a scene: a large group of people are gathered together and speaking the words of a prayer. Everyone present knows those words; they are familiar and comfortable. That blending of voices, the many speaking as one, gives a profound sense of sharing. Each person is reminded of shared values, beliefs and traditions as the prayer is intoned. Each person hears the voices of all the others around them as a powerful reminder of community and commonality. Rich and poor, old and young, come together in one voice. Some religions separate genders for prayer and ritual. People may sit in different areas, but voices may still meet and mingle in prayer. Where there is a physical component; rising, kneeling, prostrating, coming forward with offerings, there are visual reminders of commonality, too. Perhaps all around the world, members of this tradition are doing, and saying, the same things at the same sorts of times. That's a powerful, binding influence. In the joint undertaking of prayer, community is expressed, affirmed and defined.

As with so many aspects of prayer, this has little to do with esoteric belief. It is action, and the psychological impact of action, that creates an effect. Very little in our normal lives brings us into shared action with our fellows. We don't all go out into the fields to reap the harvest any more. When we lived closer to the land, and to each other, there may have been more events in our daily lives that expressed connection to community. It may be that for some of us, prayer replaces that which is otherwise missing from our lives, namely something to share with other people.

Structured prayers are full of reminders of the tradition itself. The language employed, the names mentioned, the references to values, hopes, words like "salvation", "redemption" and "duty" remind participants of core values. Our sense of the religion itself is affirmed and shored up as a consequence of praying. In this context, prayer might not be about the divine or the numinous at all. It may instead serve as a reminder of the religion, its rules, values and aspirations. The prayer becomes a poetic to-do list, a refresher course in how to behave and believe. The habit of prayer can then be a habit of paying attention to religious ideas and affirming those principles you are supposed to uphold. When prayer takes this form, it is not a spiritual practice, but a religious one. It does not take us towards personal experience, but plugs us in to the structure of an institution.

It can be warming and affirming to say words along with a bunch of other people and to have reminders of a big structure that you've opted to participate in. Wanting to belong is one of those intrinsic human drives, and can seem more important than anything else. Not to belong, is to be alone and vulnerable. There is nothing wrong with this desire. However, when we tangle social longing up with religion and spirituality, it can get messy.

Spirituality is all about personal experience. Others can guide and inspire, but no one can do it for you. Religions are full of structure and are to a large degree manifestations of culture, community and history. Formal prayers are some else's words. There can, as a consequence, be a tension between the spiritual and the social. When working inside a religious structure the need for social conformity can squash personal exploration. Working alone can be isolating and lonely. There is no one right answer here, but being alert to that inevitable tension, we can at least consider how to approach it, rather than being at its mercy.

Some traditions demand more conformity and submission than others. It is well worth considering what happens when your words of prayer are chosen by someone else. It might be one thing to pray for those suffering in war, but what happens when you are told to pray for blessings upon the guns? We might comfortably pray that politicians be blessed with wisdom and sound judgment, but what happens when our religious superiors demand that we pray for a specific legislative outcome? It's not a big step from there to being told to pray who should win the election and, by extension, who to vote for.

There is a lot of power in being able to tell someone else what to pray for. You are telling that other person what to want and how to feel about things. When that instruction comes from a religious leader, it implies that certain things fit with the religion, and often that others do not. God hates the enemy. God loves the state. History is littered with the outcomes of dragging deities into politics. If you believe in a religious institution, and that institution tells you to pray for the deaths of "undesirable" people, what effect will that have on your real-world actions?

Religious leaders are people. They have political opinions. They will have all kinds of preferences and beliefs that may be a natural extension of said religion, or may not. It may be that having already decided God is on their side, they conclude that their every prejudice has divine sanction, and preach accordingly. If you hear doctrines of hatred, violence, intolerance or advocating cruelty, you can fairly assume this process is well under way.

Bigots who believe God is on their side are only more dangerous than any other kind of bigot when they have a power source to tap into. Being able to stand up in public and tell people what to pray for, is a source of power.

It can be comfortable and pleasing to take religious inspiration from someone else. As people, we respond to charismatic leaders and simple solutions. Especially when that allows us to blame someone else for every wrong, real and imagined. This is lazy, irresponsible thinking and an attempt at abdicating responsibility. When we let ourselves be fooled into thinking someone else is more spiritual and therefore more right, we are in trouble. It is so easy to fake insight and to dress prejudice up in the language of belief. We have a personal responsibility for everything we say and do. If you go along with the intentions of the robed guy at the front, you have made a choice and are responsible for it.

If other people are writing your prayers for you, don't assume those people are better than you. Think about what the words mean, don't just chant along. All prayers are human and made by humans. There is no respect being paid to the divine when too much faith is placed in human constructions.

Social Aspects

What happens if we attend religious gatherings for social reasons? If we go along with the prayers for the sake of fitting in, but hold no personal belief? We give time, energy and our presence to something we do not believe in. We reinforce the power of a structure we don't really engage with. At best we aren't doing ourselves much good. I recall from my distant college days a tutor suggesting that one of the main reasons people are attracted to religions, is for the social aspect and the sense of belonging.

Last winter, I went to a Mediaeval Baebes concert in Gloucester cathedral. A woman ascended the pulpit before the music started, and told us we would pray. As I always do in such situations, I lowered my head to patiently wait it out in silence, respectfully not participating. Eventually, she said, "Amen."

Silence filled the cathedral, as some hundreds of people sat in the respectful silence of non-participation. I felt stunned, barely able to believe what had happened. I've sat in prayers before and felt little energy, but the raw power of that silence was memorable. There may be a moral to this story: to do nothing, with total conviction may be more effective than actions we do not invest in.

Community

I've been writing this chapter from the perspective that what we are told to believe, may influence us. No doubt, some of us are more susceptible to that, than others.

There is a great deal to be said in favour of community cohesion. We function better as individuals when we have the emotional support that comes from belonging somewhere. Societies in the west seem increasingly fragmentary. There's a tension between personal freedom, and group membership. From the outside, it looks to me as though the most substantial communities often have the most fundamentalist attitudes. It takes a power structure to make people conform to the rules needed for a tightly defined community. When there is no one who has the power to make us show up and do communal things, a lot of us simply choose not to show up. My great grand-mother had to claim a kind of social claustrophobia to duck out of church attendance, but by the time it came to my mother and I, no excuses were even required. It used to be the case that your employer could require you to show up to church. Larger communities made that impossible to monitor and so the industrial revolution eventually made attendance a bit less mandatory.

It may be that we romanticise the communities of history, simply because we've never had to live in them. I think we tend to imagine the historical village as a lovely, idyllic, cohesive place. This is probably because we weren't there. How much actual value does forced cohesion really have? An increasing lack of social contact with our fellows does not seem to be doing us any good, but this is not just a religious issue. We have lost public houses, the village shop has gone along with the village school. We are taking out a great many of the old social focal points, and we drive in our own little cars rather than walking and meeting our neighbours. People on foot can stop to chat. People in cars are isolated. It might be that social engagement issues need tackling in social ways. Without spaces for informal human contact, there is little or no scope for having a viable community. Religion can work well as part of a network of social activities, but when it is a requirement for membership of a community, I think it does far more harm than good.

When we use worship to uphold power structures (as with the example of making your employees go to church) or to force conformity, as religious fundamentalists are wont to do, religion itself is one of the first things to suffer. Making people pray is not about religion, or any kind of spiritual experience. I've sat in school assemblies and harvest festivals, weddings too, as both a child and an adult. Bring a group of people together and get them to mumble some words they barely know, don't understand and couldn't care less about, and the result is an apathetic drone. I find that has a tendency to crush rather than uplift. It is frequently the exact opposite of a spiritual experience.

One of the things I love most about Pagan circles is that the people are there only because they wanted to be. They contribute from the heart. There is no social or political advantage to showing up in a wood as a lone Pagan wanting to join in. Sometimes being "out" still runs the risk of family rejection, and social stigma. There aren't many standard Druid prayers, and I've never heard them said carelessly. It makes for a very different sort of experience.

Making people turn up and pray is unlikely to do anything for them. It may in fact put them off even further and encourage them to hate and resent what is being done, and rightly so. The presence of people who do not want to be there tends to have a negative effect on those who were keen to participate. Smaller, dedicated gatherings give participants far more than large, reluctant groups ever can. Using religion for social engineering is invariably bad news for the religion, and I don't see much evidence of it being productive on the social side, either. Using religion to promote hatred and violence is not in the interests of any religion, but does seem to be very productive in terms of the quantities of hate and violence generated. That is one of our great tragedies as a species.

Chapter Eight

Praying to Emulate

I did not plan this chapter at all, having had no awareness of the idea of emulation prayer when I started to write. Experimentation and study have continued alongside the writing process, though, so my understanding of the subject has evolved as I've been writing. Now that I am conscious of the idea of emulation through prayer, I think it is actually a widespread reason for praying, just not one that comes into the public consciousness in the way petition does. The idea of using petition to live up to religious ideals is fairly familiar. It may not be unusual to pray to a deity or a more enlightened being for help to become more like them, or more able to live up to their ideals. This approach is very much about requesting the deity acting upon you from outside, to make a petitioned change. Considered from a religious perspective, it is simply a way of asking for divine help. It may be a good deal more enlightened than asking for the oft-mentioned pony, but is still essentially a petition. Considered psychologically, praying to be changed may be viewed as reinforcing certain ideas. Thus from a position of disbelief, or no belief, prayers to acquire the virtues valued by a deity, or personified by them, may be methods of emulation.

I had not read anything about the Jain path when I first began to write about prayer. I knew it came from the same roots as Hinduism and Buddhism. There isn't a huge oral prayer tradition in Hinduism, more an emphasis on devotional acts. People can petition the gods and are expected to offer something in payment for interventions, but the topic of prayer doesn't seem to come up much. While there is a lot of similarity between devotional acts and prayer, they seem to me to be less an attempt to enter dialogue, and more an attempt to please the gods. Buddhism does included prayer as an expression of faith and compassion, and as a means to make a person more open, and otherwise seems more akin to Western prayer traditions than not. Sikhism, which emerged from the same geographical area as the aforementioned religions, uses prayer to achieve a mindfulness of God. As Jainism is one of the smaller world religions and apparently came from the same roots, I did not expect it to throw up anything different. Only later did I realise the enormity of this mistake.

Jains are nontheistic, whilst holding beliefs about reincarnation and transcending the karmic cycles of rebirth that clearly connect them to Buddhist and Hindu traditions. There are, however, a great many concepts that are specifically Jain, and one of them pertains to prayer. The figures worshipped by Jains are people who have transcended. There is an official set of these souls from ancient history, called Tirthankaras, "worshipped by Jains as symbols of omniscience [they] do not intercede on behalf of their worshippers or indeed act for humanity in any way. Instead they provide inspiration..."[22]

This instantly chimed with me, as the quest for inspiration is one of the central features of the Druid path. The same author also shares a prayer that ends with the words, "him I worship, in order that I may realise his qualities in myself."

I am interested by approaches to prayer that do not depend on belief. Methods that make rational sense, but that also enable emotional and spiritual experience seem the most significant to me. I think the idea of prayer as emulation has a great deal to offer the modern Druid. I have already mentioned the Buddhist idea that we could pray to anything, but it is not entirely clear what we might do that *for*. Emulation provides a very coherent answer. We can contemplate the qualities we wish to develop within ourselves and then consider where those manifest in nature.

What makes the Jain practice significant is the conscious way in which it is done. While emulation might be an unexpected side effect of petition in, say, Christian practice, here it is sought deliberately. Rather than understanding prayer as a means to get supernatural beings on your side, Jainism presents prayer as a spiritual-psychological tool, a means by which we change ourselves. There is no suggestion of externally sourced intervention, only that we can take inspiration by looking outside ourselves.

Worshipping that which you do not believe will intercede, as a means of finding inspiration, is something that makes a lot of sense to me. I can take this approach to a mountain, or an ocean, or any other manifestation of the natural world. Honouring, venerating, appreciating and being open to... these are modes of prayer that make more sense to me. I can't walk up to a mountain and say, *"Oi, mountain, be a dear and solve my financial problems for me."* I can walk up to the mountain and appreciate its size, and how it endures, it's solidity, and that eventually, it too will cease to exist, and then maybe decide my short-term cash flow issues aren't so critical after all.

If we take prayer to be an act of awareness, we can replace attempting to open the self to deity, with opening the self to some other source of inspiration. Letting awareness of the chosen focus fill the mind, we can simply encounter with a view to being influenced and changed. Not in the sense that something external will reshape us, but in the sense that the awareness of that other being will affect us. It requires no response or attention from the focus of prayer, only our engagement with the subject we have chosen. This is not a process that will create immediate or dramatic effects. This seems to be the case with many of the more serious approaches to prayer, so the general assumption of having a long road to walk that requires ongoing effort, is reasonable. Prayer is not about getting something for nothing (despite how atheists and New Agers alike can view the subject). Prayer is simply a tool for opening the mind and creating the scope for change.

The things we think about inform the structure of our brain and significantly impact on what we might do. My preferred example is that if you've never thought about killing your neighbour with an ice-pick, you'll probably never do that thing. However, if you consider killing your neighbour with an ice-pick on a regular basis, you are much more likely to enact the thought. Most religions seek to shape our thoughts in line with the values of said religion. Prayer is a part of that process. As Druids, we are given far less input from the tradition about how we should feel and believe. This gives us more room in which to develop our own sense of direction. We can choose who or what we wish to emulate. That could just as readily be a salmon as Ghandi, a mythical character, a river, or a season. Perhaps what we are looking for is a deeper and more meaningful expression of self. Modern life can put a lot of pressure on us to be other than we naturally are. Life experience can shift priorities away from that which we value, and leave us in need of dramatic re-thinks. The business of seeking inspiration and trying to draw closer to that which inspires us, is one way of responding to this problem.

There are advantages in having a set of Tirthankaras, saints, gurus or gods you can easily turn to for inspiration. Even if you do not anticipate these beings responding to you, emulation prayers still have room to be effective. Such prayers simply train the mind towards the chosen form. By focusing attention on the virtues, skills or traits you want to nurture in yourself, you can move towards possessing those attributes. Having a defined set of figures to work with makes it easy to know where to start. If you don't have that jumping off point, it is a bit more complicated, but still perfectly feasible as an undertaking. In part, knowing who we want to emulate requires knowing who we are. Only through being aware of our flaws and weaknesses can we see where we want to grow and change. From that awareness we might find a sense of what or who to emulate. Alternatively, in knowing ourselves, we are able to recognise that which we find inspiring, and respond to it.

I can't think of a single mythic or godlike Celtic figure I want to dedicate myself to emulating. There are plenty of characters I like reading about, but I do not like them enough to want to become as much like them as possible. The goddess Bridget with hearth, forge and poetry has a certain appeal, but she seems too Irish for me, here in the mud of the River Severn. I like Athena in her wisdom aspect, but not so much the war bit, and she is utterly foreign and I am too rooted in this landscape for that to make sense. While I empathise with Blodeuwedd probably more than I should admit, I really need to be less like her, not deep in emulating prayer. I honour Sabrina, goddess of the Severn, but she is fickle, dangerous, moody and wild. This is not the direction I wish to move in.

There are living Druids who inspire me, but there is no one I want to fully emulate there, either. Plus that would feel a tad odd, and I think any moves to semi-deify the living are likely to cause more harm than good. I'd be terrified by the idea of someone doing that to me, and am not going to act hypocritically. While I have some strong and effective women in my ancestry, and I draw inspiration from them, I don't feel any need to take that further either.

We don't really have any figures who fully embody what a modern Druid might aspire to emulate, much less anyone all Druids could agree to emulate. I draw the line at imagining my perfect example in order to then pray to them. I do not think I could suspend my disbelief enough to make that work. I find it makes more sense for me, at present, to concentrate on aspects of the natural world in the search for qualities to emulate.

I took the notion of emulation into my usual prayer work, asking the unknown for some pointers in the right direction. That night, I dreamed about dragons. There is a lot to be said in favour of dragons: they embody strength, beauty, magic and wisdom – at least for me. I associate them with elemental forces, and I like the visual imagery. On the whole that would suggest I could take the prompt from my unconscious and pray to emulate the virtues of dragons. The result was a pretty good meditation. There can be a hazy grey region between prayer and meditation. Arguably, shamanic journeying is a precise blending of the two disciplines. Most of the time I find that while I can move easily from one to the other, they remain distinctly different for me. I can meditate on the qualities of dragons, but I cannot get to grips with praying to emulate dragons.

This raises an interesting question for me around the nature of belief. I like the imagery and symbolism of dragons. Of course I want there to be real, actual dragons. As I've yet to experience a dragon, I find it hard to approach the idea of them with anything prayer-shaped. While I don't have firm belief in gods, I accept the possibility that there might be something. Apparently that was enough to make whispering "Hello?" into the darkness a viable activity. I don't really believe in dragons as something literally present, much as it pains me to admit this. That greater degree of certainty rules out scope for prayer.

The Tirthankaras of Jain tradition were, at least in theory, real people. The Buddha was supposedly one single, real bloke as well as, in theory, was Jesus. It is entirely possible that figures in myths are reflections and echoes of people who once lived. It takes just the tiniest thread of possibility to allow a small suspicion of belief. I cannot pray to emulate Harry Potter or Mr. Spock, because they are fictions and knowing that is a barrier for me. (This is just one of the many reasons why I am never going to be a chaos magician!) Rhiannon and Macha could be fictional figures as well, but I do not *know* that they are, and apparently I can suspend my disbelief that far.

If I was following a modern magical tradition, I would probably be working on dissolving those belief barriers so that I could believe anything that happened to seem useful at the time. If I embraced the notion that there is no reality, only perception and belief, I could consciously direct my belief and harness prayer as a magical tool. Plenty of people do just this, but I find it holds no attraction for me. I think this is because power becomes ever less appealing to me. I am not looking for the means to be powerful. What I want from my Druidry are trans-formative experiences. I want to grow and learn. At the same time, as an occasional author of fiction, I'm very conscious of my own ability to make stuff up. I'm not interested in locking myself into fantasies of my own creation. I want to open out, know more, and experience more. What happens in my spiritual work needs to be distinctly different from my story-making activities.

After the first ritual I attended, the chap running it mentioned his impression that you need to bring a great deal of imagination to Wicca, to make it work. I did not want that to be true. I still don't. Call it Wicca, Druidry, Islam or anything else, it still needs to be more than a let's pretend session for grownups. There are so many spiritual writers from all traditions who talk about personal experience. Can they all be imagining it or making it up? Is religion just a longstanding collective delusion? A case of the emperor with no clothes on?

All we ever get in life, is personal experience. Are we willing to believe in our own experiences? Are we willing to believe that beliefs are more than collective insanity? I want to believe that belief is meaningful.

Part of the problem around my not being able to figure out how to undertake emulation prayer, is that I lack an overall sense of direction. I am not attempting to transcend, and I've no sense that I am capable of enlightenment. I want to be more than I am, and do everything in better ways, giving more to others and causing less harm.

Dear whatever-you-ares that lurk in the fleeting, numinous moments, any chance of a pointer in the direction towards something or someone I could aspire to emulate?

But not dragons, because that didn't quite work for me.

Chapter Nine

The Practicalities of Prayer

In this chapter I'm going to step away from the more esoteric and philosophical issues for a while to think more about the practical aspects of prayer. What do we do with our minds and bodies whilst praying? What space do we need, what physical resources? Practices from other traditions give us ideas to consider, but how should a Druid go about praying? As ours is a non-dogmatic faith, the first priority must be that the method makes both intellectual and emotional sense to the person using it. Anything that feels awkward, foolish or irrelevant will be of little use.

When?

Some religions offer set times for prayer. It's not unusual for dedicants – monks, nuns, priests, ascetics and the like – to have more rigorously scheduled prayer routines than do lay people. That also includes whether you have set prayer times. Lay people can have fixed prayer routines too – Islam with its multiple Friday prayer sessions being an example of this.

Obvious candidates for prayer time are: after waking, just before sleep, and around mealtimes. These imbed prayer practice in the practical structure of the day. Setting aside certain times of the day based on the clock can be an option, and lifestyles may suggest other points in time that can be meaningfully framed with prayer. In a community dedicated to the spiritual life, prayer and practicality intertwine. For the lay person it is more likely the case that either time is made at some point for prayer, or that prayer doesn't feature in any structured way, outside of formal gatherings for worship. The Sunday prayers of Christianity could be an example of this.

It is perfectly reasonable to take an informal approach and pray only when it occurs to you to do so. However, a person who wants a prayer practice as part of their spiritual life will probably need to consider something a bit more structured. There is a lot to be said for dedicating a small period of time on a daily basis. Not least, anything we do every day rapidly becomes a habit and therefore is easier to maintain than something sporadic. Praying on a daily basis creates a rhythm of its own, and rapidly takes you away from petition. Praying when it occurs to you is more likely to take the form of petition because we may be more likely to pray when we feel we need something to happen. Coming to prayer day after day does tend to create some impetus towards finding new ideas to pray with. If anyone is listening, there's nothing to be gained by boring them witless! I find that daily prayer (or most days, at least) keeps me paying attention to what I am doing this for. This in turn keeps me alert to not whining on about what's bothering me and what I want to have work out in my favour. With a daily prayer habit, I notice when I'm obsessing over the same things repeatedly, and this helps me to better manage my own thoughts.

I have not tried a prayer pattern that calls for sessions throughout the day. Partly there is a practical time issue. I'm not cloistered in a monastery. I am a person with a family and other work to do. There is also the issue of potentially becoming too involved with prayer and taking myself out of the world too much. Having had problems around that early on, I feel a need to be mindful of the balance between wholly spiritual work and the rest of life, and to avoid excess. A person wishing to adopt a more monastic lifestyle will want a more involved discipline. We all have different needs and intentions, so the important thing is to work out what those are and act accordingly.

One critical consideration around "when" is the need for some quiet time. Prayer requires your attention. You might not choose to devote many minutes, but those need to be free from interruption. Finding quiet times and spaces may be the defining factor around when and how you pray. If your life entirely lacks that kind of space, consider making changes. Whatever we are doing, quiet time is essential for all aspects of life, not just spirituality. We all need space to breathe, moments of tranquillity, and a little scope to be alone with the self. This is not just a prayer issue, but a basic sanity and wellbeing issue.

How long you spend praying may depend on what time you have to spare. How long you can consciously engage with praying will be an issue too. Your concentration span and having material to pray with both inform that. Both will improve with practise. There is no point pushing beyond what you can comfortably sustain. If prayer becomes a chore, that can be a barrier to getting anything positive out of doing it. Unlike followers of some faiths, we do not have gods who require us to show up and worship on a regular basis. We don't get points for sitting there trying to pray, nor do we get points for suffering. There is nothing to be gained from boredom, frustration, irritation and the like. If you are unhappy, it may be as well to quit and come back another time. Discipline does not mean slogging away for no discernible reason.

Experiment with how long you pray for, and see what suits you. You may find that you spend different amounts of time in prayer on different days. It is worth considering what inspires you towards prayer and what creates disinterest – it is useful self-knowledge and will help you build a way of working that actually answers your needs. You may find there are patterns of influence informing your prayer work, from both within and from your surroundings. If contact with an individual leaves you too irritable to pray, there might be things in your life in need of attention. If a long swim enables a rewarding prayer session, that might influence how you structure your time. While we all respond to different things, coming to prayer in a state of anger or frustration isn't ideal. The prayer work may settle you but that's probably the best you can hope for. Coming to prayer when you already feel relaxed or in a good mood tends to be more effective. Too much enthusiasm, drama, energy or excitement can be a distraction.

Some of the issues around approaching prayer can be dealt with by using meditation techniques first. Soothing the mind before attempting to pray requires more time, and the willingness to move away from emotional distractions to seek a quiet state. Taking the drama in life and praying for resolution can have the effect of drawing your mind deeper into all the consternation, rather than helping you move away from it. There are times when we need to pause and really look at what is happening, to have any hope of sorting it out. There are other times when our investment in a drama is what keeps it energised. When that happens, the most productive thing can be to step away. There are no absolutes here because every situation is different. The only thing I will put forward as a certainty is that an overly busy head is not helpful for prayer, and also isn't likely to be helped much by praying.

How?

In terms of how we deploy the body, how do we pray? The trend across the world faiths is towards postures of submission; on our knees, head bowed, bringing our face to the floor. Then there are more extreme methods that call for difficult and uncomfortable positions. With these, adopting the position can be seen as an act of worship, and we might understand yoga in those terms, for example. A Christian who prays in a crucified position (more popular historically than today) is literally aligning themselves with Christ. A Heathen might take the same sort of position in reference to Odin hanging from the world tree, perhaps.

How we hold our bodies influences our minds. Thus the slumped posture of apathy and defeat reinforces those feelings in a depressed person. Posturing reinforces a sense of power; the strutting about, taking up space and looming over people expresses authority to the posturer as well as to the victim. Whether we hold our bodies open, with loose arms and exposed chest, or whether we fold ourselves into a protective ball, both influences and reflects mood. If you are unconvinced by the theory, try testing it on yourself.

The usual physical approach to prayer is to be humble and submissive before deity. This involves making the body seem small, and avoiding any position that suggests power or action. Further, in communal prayer, we make ourselves the same as everyone else around us who bends, kneels or otherwise expresses submission. There can be something good about this, especially for people who do not normally get to feel small and powerless in their lives, and who need some balance. Nature and the universe are much bigger than us. Time, history, humanity, infinity – we should know ourselves to be utterly dwarfed by these things. Mostly we live as emperors of our inner realms, trying to ignore our smallness. A little perspective can be highly beneficial.

The humble position may encourage a humble mind; one able to be overwhelmed by everything outside of the self. However, that might not be what is happening. Kindly envisage this, or try it: You are kneeling with your head bowed. If you have your eyes open, you can see a few square feet of ground. If your eyes are closed, you are entirely inside your own mind. Right now, either way, you are the centre of a tiny world. Furthermore, the posture of submission you have adopted is, really speaking, the posture of submitting to another human being. You would feel that keenly if someone else entered the scene and stood over you, posturing power. This is the position we take up when dealing with tyrants. Without any immediate, personal looming, you have to imagine deity into the same space. What you can see are a few features of the immediate floor and the lower halves of anyone close by. If you get a personal revelation of deity in that moment, all well and good, but I suspect the majority feel little more than discomfort to the knees.

My reasoning around this is as follows. The all-powerful, all knowing gods who preside over these forms of prayer in other traditions, are so vast that exposure to them can hardly be comfortable. Would we really kneel down with a bunch of other people if we expected to feel the crushing enormity of the infinite? I think when we undertake this kind of prayer it is precisely because we do not feel the enormity of deity. Instead, we are putting ourselves into a safe position to imagine what kneeling before an all-powerful being would be like.

Opportunities to truly experience humble awe in the face of enormity are not to be found looking down at a nearby floor. Try looking up, instead. Specifically, try looking up on a clear night and taking a while to contemplate the uncountable stars strewn across the sky. Then consider the light years of distance between the stars, and the age of the light you are perceiving. Consider what your life means to those stars and what difference your actions make to the barely comprehensible span of time and space now visible to you. When you feel giddy and it seems as though you could fall into the abyss at any moment, falling to your knees will be a relief. Then you might want to bow your head for the sheer comfort of looking at the earth and considering something manageably small.

There is no official posture for Pagan prayer. Often, in Druid ritual when evocations are offered to the four directions, participants stand with their arms open wide. Hands can be either at waist height in this gesture, or raised towards the sky, at whatever height appeals. Interestingly, both the hands at waist height and hands above head positions are akin to Chi Quong exercises – standing meditations from the Taoist tradition. Taoism and its physical expression, Tai Chi, is all about opening up to the flow of the universe. Standard prayer positions, especially from monotheism, are actually quite closed. Hands together, heads down, bodies folded up, there is no room for anything to get in. Perhaps that closing down of the body helps someone who wants to transcend the flesh, and attune themselves to spirit. This has little relevance for many Druids. The only answer is to experiment and find out what works for you. There doesn't have to be one right way at an individual level, either, just so long as what you do makes sense to you at the time.

Prayer requires mental focus. If you are physically uncomfortable, this will create a distraction. If you cannot stand comfortably, then don't stand. If your best position for being free of bodily grumbles is horizontal, then lie down. Trying to fight your body is not conducive to prayer. It is also important to be free from distractions and interruptions. That means liberating yourself from technology and the demands of others. If that means praying whilst in the shower, that's fine.

Some traditions have pre-prayer rituals as well. Washing seems to be the most usual, although this can be more symbolic than literal. A dabble in some water for a few chosen body parts is apparently enough. I wonder if this grew out of rituals that were more literally about making the body clean. Fasting and other forms of abstention also feature. The degree of complexity in the pre-prayer ritual tends to depend on the importance of the event and the status of the person undertaking it. A lay person might only do something complicated a couple of times a year for key events. A dedicated monk or priest might go through complex rituals on a daily basis. Any aspect of normal life can be co-opted as part of a pre-prayer ritual, depending on need and inclination. The point of such activities is to help us step out of our normal modes of being and adopt an appropriate state of mind for what is ahead.

When it comes to preparation work, Druidry has no rules. However, one thing to consider is the relationship between our spiritual life and our mundane life. Many religions aim to transcend the world. Druidry does not. Therefore, we more often seek to bring the spiritual into daily life. To what extent do we want to ritually transition out of normal life in order to pray? Granted, some calm is necessary, but how removed do we wish to be? My feeling is that in an ideal world, we would always be acting in ways that are conducive to prayer, and supported by environments that do not preclude spiritual activity. This would mean living free from physical violence and psychological abuse, having a healthy relationship with our own emotions, self-control, a default of inner peacefulness and some freedom in how we live. Ideals are one thing, reality quite another. The strains of existing naturally are not at odds with being prayerful, but the ways in which humans treat each other leaves us with much less space for spiritual life. All too often we are not allowed to go slowly, or to think things through, we are subject to unnecessary pressure and harassment, unreasonable demands and unhealthy situations.

I do think it pays to look at how much transition work we need to do in order to reach a state of being able to pray. The harder it is to achieve a calm, inner state, the more issues we have, and it may be that attention given to our wider lives would be more productive in that case, than trying to pray when little around us supports that.

Where?

In theory of course, anyone can pray anywhere. The big advantage of temples and other established places, is that they have atmospheres conducive to prayer. You can expect peace, respect, and a mood that supports what you do. This makes it easy to transition into a suitable state of mind. Lighting, music, décor, incense and habitual religious use all contribute to reinforcing the idea of prayer. I will admit that I like going into cathedrals to pray, for all of these reasons. It is a curious irony that often my little Druid family are the only people to be using the cathedral in a sacred way, when we visit. Others seem to be there to work, which is fair enough, or are tourists, or there for some educational purpose. Increasingly, cathedrals seem to be charging for entry, offering themselves as places of amusement. Apparently we are more interested in museum pieces and tourist attractions than we are in the spiritual function of such buildings.

Some of the ancient Pagans built temples to worship in, but the general perception seems to be that Druids worshipped in groves of trees. The Celts used wooden buildings that leave little evidence, and the business of groves comes to us from after the arrival of the Romans. It is therefore entirely possible that pre-Roman Druids did something else entirely. There are no surviving Druid temples at any rate. They may have used stone circles like Stonehenge, but that would be a case of adopting something older. Although the other argument is that Druidry evolved out of the religions that built the henges and circles. We might take inspiration from this, and many modern Druids do use ancient sites. However, many Druids are not in Europe, some are in landscapes that do not support groves of trees even. We have to work with whatever we've got.

For modern Pagans of all kinds, a personal shrine within the home may be the best answer to the need for dedicated space. Many do not feel this need at all – nature is our temple, and outside is plenty sacred enough. There are many beautiful places in which to celebrate. Where you choose to go should mainly be informed by where you find resonance and a sense of connection. If you want a sacred space, but do not have a private space to use, then getting out on foot, or otherwise without a car, is the best way. Travelling in a way that involves you with the landscape, and moves you slowly, gives you a far better chance of finding somewhere that could be a sacred space for you. Setting out to look is the first stage in making a relationship with the space.

There are Pagans who attempt to make shrines in their preferred public space. Fruit, tea lights, dead flowers, even plastic items find their way to iconic locations, and once they start to decay become nothing more than litter. We should be able to do better than this, to which end I have some suggestions. Why not make a portable shrine, an altar cloth, candles, incense, wands, or whatever else you like, all wrapped up for ease of carrying, and then wrapped once more to be taken away after use. Alternatively, you could collect naturally occurring items from the space you are in – fallen leaves, feathers, twigs and stones (no need to kill anything) and assemble them into a temporary altar that can be left to return to chaos. You do not cause problems to a place if you work gently with what is in it already.

If you feel the need to make offerings, consider what the place has a need for. Do not introduce alien things just because they look pretty. The best offerings are often those of effort, taking away other people's litter, especially. The detritus of other, less considerate Pagans should be of particular priority.

By repeatedly using the same space for prayer, you can build a relationship with it. If you are seeking spirits of place or gods of the land, nothing beats going to where they are. It is a gesture of respect, it also gives you more scope for encountering the real as opposed to your imagination. This tree, that rock, not a make believe.

Chapter Ten

Attitudes to Prayer

There is a flow of influence between where we go to in order to pray, how we utilise our bodies once there, and the emotions and expectations we bring to prayer. If these harmonise, we will have a much better experience than if we feel conflict. For example, if we are obliged to pray somewhere we don't much like, if our bodies provide obstacles, or ambivalence of belief gets in the way, there will be no glorious outcome. This is fine, and if you run into such issues, it is simply an invitation to take a deeper look. Most things in life require practice and some fine tuning to discover what suits us best. If prayer does not work in the way you want it to, then assess your physical arrangements and feelings to work out what needs to change. Then make those changes, or at least work towards them.

Being on a spiritual path changes a person, and being changed is very much part of the point in any of this work. What I needed from Druidry ten years ago has very little in common with what I find I need today. Life changes us. Druidry changes life, and what was valuable before can become meaningless. When we first come to prayer, and to a wider spiritual tradition, we most likely come along wanting something: peace, enlightenment, importance, hope... There are many things to want.

Blessed Kami, I just want someone to love me... hail spirits of place, let me be The Druid of this sacred grove... Dear Gods, make it stop hurting...

We are human, driven by wants and needs that come from our experience of life. This is what we bring to prayer. There is no shame in this. You can only show up with what you have. If you were peace-laden and enlightened already, there would be no need to show up and no further work to do.

We pray out of our needs and wants. This is a process which begins from wherever you are, regardless of where that is in relation to anyone else. I do not think there is much point fretting over where you imagine you are "supposed" to be. Many mainstream religions advocate turning up with a specific attitude. Submission to god, a worshipful approach, an open heart, a sense of gratitude, or a feeling of humbleness, are all recommended. There is a definite sense that turning up in the petulant child mind-set of *I want a pony* is not acceptable. However, this may well be where we start.

I came to prayer in a state of pain and fear. I was ill of body and mind as a direct consequence of experiences both historical and on-going. My trust was impaired... *and dammit gods, I could use some help sorting this out.* Had I started out more able to believe in both prayer and deity, I would have petitioned with those needs and wants, probably to the exclusion of all else. As I didn't see much point in petition, those *for pity's sake, make this stop* prayers came only in extremity. Admittedly, there were a lot of times when I was in some agonising and impossible positions. I can't say that desperate moments of petition helped me in the slightest.

I suspect it doesn't really matter where we start. We ask, and we approach, offering up pain and need, doubt, curiosity, or whatever else we have. Mostly no one answers. This should bring anyone who prays to a crisis point. Prayer isn't solving your problems, or adding to your life much, so do you quit, or continue? To get past this crisis, you need to hold the attitude that, even if you aren't getting tangible results, there is some point to prayer. Something is happening, even if you can't perceive it yet. If you believe you are learning and changing, that will carry you forward. If you believe the act of showing up to pray means something, regardless of apparent outcome, you can keep doing it. If all you wanted was the pony, now is the time to give up. There may be people for whom a result manifests – by some means – who then feel a belief in the effectiveness of petition. I assume the first crisis will simply turn up later for them, whenever petition first definitively fails them.

It may be that over time, the wants and needs that first created the urge to pray are changed by a shift in perspective. The desire to bother deity with trivia should reduce as we become more settled in ourselves and more able to accept that we can't have magic solutions. This can work with more serious life issues, too. Learning how to recognise and accept the inevitable is part of spiritual growth. That in turn enables us to focus our energy on things that can be changed, which makes it more feasible to create changes. Maybe you start seeing how to change things for yourself, or start to focus on the more positive aspects of your life. The process of reflection can bring many benefits without any need for divine intervention. This can lead us to a second crisis, which is more subtle and likely to happen as a process, not an event. You have become calmer and more realistic about life. You get on with dealing with things, you take responsibility. What do you need prayer for? If you have found what was needed and the job is done, why not move on? Again, we come back to attitude. To keep going, you need a sense that prayer is more than problem solving and that there is some other level to it, some reason to keep showing up.

There is a dance here, a process of needing less and showing up to pray anyway, and I've been conscious of this one for a while now. As my expectations become more realistic, I cope better with life. As I make the necessary changes to protect myself and improve my lot, the need for magical solutions decreases. What has happened to me has not been a stripping away of optimism, or a giving up on cherished dreams, but a process of learning to think better of people than I did. I no longer assume that the bad experiences I've had are typical of what I can expect from reality. That allows me to be more open, more engaged with life rather than closed and defensive. This has resulted in making ever less petition, but showing up to pray anyway, and accepting that little appears to be happening most of the time. Except that there has been a discernible shift going on within me and looking back the significance of it is considerable. As I change, my behaviour changes, my choices change, and I become other than I was. Many changes – like getting fit or losing weight – are not evident from one day to the next, but over a space of months can represent a dramatic shift in my sense of wellbeing.

I think a sense of encountering something that responds when you pray could create another crisis point. If we start to hear voices, or have a real sense of presence, then by any normal measure, that suggests a total failure of the mind. At some point it may be necessary to choose whether to accept your experiences as a valid reality, or reject them as insane. Why pray in the first place if you are not open to having your reality change? Why appeal to the universe, in any of its manifestations, if you do not want the universe to speak back to you? There can be a great deal of difference between imagining an experience, and having it happen. Rape fantasies are not the same as a desire to actually be raped. Perhaps we have deity fantasies that are not the same as a desire to actually encounter something on that scale.

Thus far I've mostly been exploring our attitudes to ourselves and how that affects us in prayer, although as the final thought above flags up, our attitude to the divine is also an issue to consider. Some Pagans report entering into very personal, intimate and chummy relationships with specific deities. For others, gods remain wholly mysterious and largely unreachable. To what degree is this a reflection of the nature of the deity involved? To what degree is this relationship something that happens inside a person's head, as a product of imagination? How important is the nature of the deity in shaping this, assuming they exist independently and are present in the relationship? Go back to the myths of the ancient Mediterranean and you can find figures who are supposed to be children of gods and mortals, which suggests even greater degrees of intimacy than we moderns will claim.

This issue of how people have relationships with the divine is one which transcends the boundaries between religions. There are those who have a personal relationship with Jesus, those who need to go through his mother, those who need to petition a saint to talk to Mary so that she can talk to Jesus for them... We use all kinds of religious figures – priests, semi-divine beings and the dead to mediate on our behalf. It doesn't seem to be the case that the deity defines the way in which they can be related to. However, if we consider levels of intimacy and availability in purely human relationships, another possibility emerges. There are people whose doorsteps I could turn up at with no notice and expect a warm reception. There are others who do not know me and whose responses I therefore cannot predict. I can think of a few people who would be entirely hostile if I came to their door. The kind of relationship we seek will inform, to a degree, what we get, or imagine we get in both human and divine contexts. It may be fair to assume that deities have their own feelings and preferences too, more willing to show up at some sites than others, more attracted by certain kinds of rituals or activities, more or less open to prayer and so forth. All relationships are a connection between two things, or beings, with scope for input on both side. And so Jesus doesn't talk to me at all, which is just as well because I'd be deeply disconcerted if he did.

Is this, really speaking, an attitude issue? Does our relationship with the divine come down to our own beliefs and perceptions? It is nigh on impossible to see things you aren't looking for and do not believe exist. As I've never sought a personal relationship with Thor, it should come as no surprise that he's never tried to communicate with me either. Is that about me, or him? I won't know unless I try praying to Thor, but that of course changes things anyway. I have heard various Pagans express the feeling that a deity has chosen them. This is not something I've experienced, but it is so often reported that it merits considerable reflection. The experience of being god-bothered can be unsought and unexpected, such a surprise to the one on the receiving end that it can take them a while to take it seriously and respond. This suggests the possibility of a two-way flow of interest. The role of the individual's attitude may be considerable, but is hard to assess. We either experience inter-acting with deity personally, or stand on the outside observing someone else talking about what happens to them. Either way, the relationship between desire and outcome might not be easy to trace. We aren't always fully conscious of our own motives, much less anyone else's.

Our attitude to deity, our understanding of it, and our relationship with it are all informing each other and collectively shaping how we interpret experiences in an ongoing way. If you do not believe in deity, you will not interpret an experience as demonstrating the presence of deity. Equally, if you start from a place of belief, you will be more likely to see the influence of deity in your life. Those of us who are intrinsically uncertain may just have to settle for not knowing because we will never quite trust our own judgment enough to either believe, or disbelieve.

This brings me back to questions from the very start of the book. To whom do we pray? It is not the identity of the deity that shapes our experiences. Do we see deity as close, personal and available, or vast, remote and unreachable? This will inform what we get, to at least some degree. During the research stage for this book, I talked to a Christian woman who explained to me that she prayed as though she was talking to her own father, taking a chatty, personal and deeply intimate approach to prayer. Formal prayers can suggest a less personal sense of deity. This in turn can also be a reflection of how we conduct our human relationships with authority, I suspect. We probably take many of our everyday life assumptions to deity: obsequious, demanding, fearful or friendly, perhaps we play out our usual relationship with power, in prayer. Or perhaps the process is circular, with the way we are taught to, or inclined to, consider deity also informing how we respond to authority generally.

The overlap between religious and secular power makes this a very interesting consideration. To what degree do attitudes to gods shape attitudes to secular authority? Based on anecdotal evidence, atheists seem highly resistant to all arbitrary expressions of power. They like decision-making based on evidence, reason and democratic process. Pagans tend not to be keen on authority either (excepting those odd Pagans who want to be an authority themselves). Again, from anecdotal evidence, I think a lot of Pagans have a more personal sense of relationship with deity, fostering more intimate and improvised approaches. It is my impression that those people who are most keen to force their religious rules upon others are also those who perceive deity as tyrannical and merciless. If you are fundamental about your religion, the odds are that you aren't liberal about anything else, either. I am largely convinced that there is a very direct link between how we feel about the authority of gods, and how we feel about authority in general. There is, as a consequence, a distinctly political dimension to religion.

There may be wider cultural aspects to this issue as well. I live in a place and time that lacks formality. Use of first names is normal, there are no "sirs" or "madams" in normal exchanges. We feel less respect for titles than we did in the past, and this all contributes to how we might think about divine authority. Go back a hundred years or so and the etiquette around status and authority was clearly defined. Formal prayer through regular church attendance was also more usual. There may be causality at work here, but it would be hard to say in which direction, and I suspect it is in fact a circular process. I think the loss of formality goes more generally with the de-ritualising and individualising of life, and with weakening social bonds. We have come to see formality as stuffy and old fashioned, but communities make rituals to reinforce relationships. The loss of formality can mean a loss of connection. Equally, an informal approach to prayer, or any other spiritual activity for that matter, can mean neglect.

Many modern Pagans favour ritual – sometimes scripted, usually following an established pattern. For all that we tend not to like authority, we do like certain formalities. *Hail and welcome, merry meet, so mote it be and blessed be...* Existing as a small and relatively vulnerable community tucked into a much larger culture, we favour the rituals of community cohesion. In looks and speech, we like to be identifiably "us". Clearly there are a number of different impulses at play here, none of them entirely unrelated to each other.

We are, here in the west, a lot less open to the idea of deity than we used to be. This is to a large extent because acting on the instructions voiced by God can be a one-way ticket to incarceration in a mental institution. It may be socially acceptable to pray, but getting an answer is largely off-limits. We can ask things of the gods with impunity, but if we in any way admit we think those prayers are being answered, we join the lunatic fringe in many people's eyes. This is not especially tempting. It is also a new development, when you consider how much of human history has not included taboos around acknowledging the supernatural. This leaves us praying for things whilst having a vested interest in not seeing or hearing any kind of answer. This is not an attitude to prayer likely to achieve meaningful results. It is socially excusable to pray if you can treat it as being just a form of meditation and a mental exercise, but otherwise it is only truly permissible as a gesture of social engagement. To pray with the intention of getting a response, is to be crazy, a fundamentalist, an affront to reason...

Dear God, of whom I ask nothing in particular, please note that I have shown up wearing a nice hat in your honour, just in case there turns out to be an afterlife. Please bless me, but not too much, so that I am not obliged to recognise it, as that would be embarrassing.

The necessity of failing is often hardwired into the attitude we bring to prayer. We need it not to work. If the gods answered, it would mean we were insane, or at best, weird. There have been times and there are still places where it is or was socially acceptable to hear the gods. In such contexts, people hear gods. Maybe that is just a consequence of socially approved wishful thinking. Perhaps it is all about a way to seek power and attention. Hearing gods, in the right context, could be a real boost to your career. We could put it down to collective fear or mass hallucination, perhaps. Those mediaeval folk drank a lot of beer and were frequently ill, which may have messed with their perceptions. In all things, we tend to find what we were looking for and ignore that which we do not believe. Neither of these has anything to do with objective reality. Assuming an objective reality exists.

I don't think it matters in the slightest whether you pray formally to the unreachable or want a friendly chat with a mother goddess, or something in between. The key feature to holding a "right attitude" is willingness to get a result. If you do not want to hear voices, or to have prayers answered in other ways, don't go there. Stick to meditation, which will deliver what you need without any of the messy, irrational bits. Nothing can be gained from prayer that exceeds what meditation delivers, if you entirely disbelieve the process, or you fear the possible outcomes. If you aren't willing to change then don't pray. If you aren't willing to be confused, frightened, overwhelmed or intimidated sometimes, don't pray.

If you get prayer to work for you, then at times it will be neither wholly safe nor wholly comfortable. Just undertaking to pray changes your relationship with reality. It takes you away from the safely rational into activities some people will have a problem with. Prayer taken seriously can threaten your place in the social order. Many religions have tamed prayer, putting it into books and buildings that enable us to go safely through the motions without actually feeling anything. True prayer is wilder in nature. It is not controlled and dependable, and there can be risks, but mostly in a good way. Life, after all, is a risky business and only the dead seem free from pressures to change.

Chapter Eleven

A Mind Full of Prayer

Mostly we are alone in our heads. To a large extent, prayer is an invitation for something else to come in from the outside. This bears thinking about properly. We are used to thinking of ourselves as being alone inside our skulls. We are also automatous, independent beings, and our minds are utterly private places in which we have total control. Are you willing to give any of that up?

The classic image of prayer has the person saying their words out loud, the divine hearing, and God (probably voiced by some bloke with a booming voice from a 1950s movie) replying. It's all very external and real-world. In that set-up, the person praying is in no doubt about what has happened: they heard God. He probably had some backing singers and nice lighting effects to further clarify the point. Are you looking for that kind of prayer experience? If that happened to you, would you assume you had gone mad? Could you trust an experience of that nature? We return to the issue of attitude. Do we expect the gods to literally hear us and audibly respond? I have never had a first-hand experience like that, nor do I know anyone who admits to anything in that vein. That kind of religious experience is "old-school" and belongs to a world that had not yet invented reason or scientific method.

Perhaps the gods did show up in person in the ancient world. Do we want that to happen now? Are you hoping Odin, Cernunos or Bast will literally and definitively manifest before your eyes in response to a prayer? Or do you suppose (as I do) that this would be a situation likely to result in instant bowel failure? As it happens, I did once meet a young lady who claimed she could cause Bast to manifest. Part of me wanted to see, but it turned out that most of me really, really didn't. I was a lot younger at the time, but wise enough to know I preferred not to encounter an ancient Egyptian deity, whilst holding to the possibility that the girl was telling the truth. Not only did I want not to see, but I certainly didn't want to find there was nothing to see. By such means do we protect ourselves.

I suspect all manner of things were different for our ancient Pagan ancestors. In a society steeped in belief, where seeing gods does not mark you out as deranged, it may have been a lot easier to encounter the divine. That takes us back to those issues about what makes a spiritual experience. Whether this is a thing of the mind, a state of awareness or an encounter with something external is hard to say, but no matter what it is, most things are more easily done in a context that supports them. We do not invest much effort in things we assume are impossible. I think that, due to the context most of us live in, our modern minds would not handle the kinds of spiritual experiences our ancestors might have considered normal. This may in turn be a part of why our experiences so often differ from the reports of our ancestors. While they probably feared the gods, we fear the idea of gods, and even our religions are structured to keep us safe from experiencing too much.

Now, let's step away from this line of speculation, and backtrack into your head. My head. That safe and private inner space we all have. Do you want anyone else in there with you? My voice may be landing in your brain via these phrases, but I can't see what you're thinking. If I could, it would probably make you uncomfortable. How much more uncomfortable would it be to have the invasive presence be something bigger and more powerful than yourself? Something that, once it gets in, you may not be able to remove. Something that could control you. If deity is not going to manifest dramatically outside your skin, then it's going to show up inside your head. Voices inside your head... and we know what that means. Should that happen you will either have to start disbelieving in your own experience, which is crazy, or believe it, which is also crazy. Either way, you are bound to step out of consensus reality, out of the normal world of the people around you. Talk about this kind of experience, even with other spiritual people, and you run the risk they will think you are losing the plot. Carry such an experience alone and unsupported, and you might well lose the plot anyway.

The more I think about it, the more I wonder if this is the point of most religions – to provide a structure that gives us formal ways to approach deity that will also safeguard our sanity by not letting us actually get there.

Our Father who art conveniently a very long way away, kindly stay there and do not alarm us this day with anything we are going to have a hard time explaining…

What would any of us become, if we knew that we could interact with deity regularly and perhaps at will? Regardless of whether deity exists by any objective measure, what does that quest do to us? Lunatics or poets all. Not that there is always much difference between the two. Just by undertaking to do something like this, our understanding of life and our place in it would be bound to change. Our relationship with worldly authorities would change too. How would we live? Take a step further and postulate that the open, faithful and willing one is able to get a tangible response from deity, and imagine the consequences. It would be difficult to live with, to say the least.

I suspect the exact impact would vary greatly. Whether or not we could bear to consider how our own lives measure up in face of such absolutes, would be an issue. Then, the kind of gods we find (or think we find) would have profound effects on our life choices. Considering the shocking cruelties carried out in the name of religion, we might wonder at the deities inspiring murder around the world. What if we discovered that the gods exist, and that they are all the hellfire and damnation fundamentalists could wish them to be? That might explain a few things. I also wonder about the kind of personal experience necessary to confirm, in more than just an intellectual way, that there is no deity. A revelation of no-god, as a spiritual experience, could be as overwhelming as any other spiritual experience we might have. If one person has that enlightening no-deity revelation, another sees the gods of slaughter, and a third finds gods of harmony, do any of those experiences disprove, or affirm the others? Not really.

While I've heard atheists claim that we are born atheists and taught belief, I'm not inclined to agree with this. We are born wondering and questioning. Experience, observation and the answers offered by other people may give us ways of dealing with those questions. Sometimes those answers are good enough for us to be comfortable with. *Why is the grass green and where do butterflies come from?* might be easy enough to tackle. *What does life mean?* keeps us on our toes. We throw human words, human numbers and ideas at the enormity of the universe, and miraculously, some of it sticks and makes passable sense. We are small. For me "gods" are increasingly that which I cannot get my head round, that which shapes and informs my life but is mostly beyond my comprehension. There's a lot of it out there.

In trying to be more open to the possibility of deity, I have experienced changes in my mind. I have become more open to other people, willing to imagine the best rather than the worst of them. Compared to how I was when I started, I am a good deal calmer and better able to hold boundaries. I feel that I have less to prove than I did, but have also become more able to take action when necessary, and less dependent on outcomes to inform my mental well-being. That in turn makes me tougher and more capable. I trust my own judgment more than I used to, I trust the value of my own work and the accuracy of my intuition. When the good in what I do is not immediately reflected back to me in the feedback of others, I am less undermined by this than I used to be. I feel that I'm doing the work I need to be doing, bit by bit, and that certainty changes a lot of things for me. I perceive my choices as rational, well founded and productive. For the first time in my life I am able to consider the possibility that if someone doesn't like what I'm doing, that's their problem, not mine.

I am not ascribing all of this to the power of prayer. There have been many influences in my life over the last year or so. At the same time, it would be pretty irrational to expect prayer to exist in isolation, given the interconnected nature of existence. Ripples of causality flow in all kinds of directions. Often flows of influence can be circular, for good or ill. As much as anything else, I think taking the time to do something determinedly positive has changed how I relate to myself, and from there all else changes. Maybe there's a divine influence in the mix, maybe there isn't. The more I use words like "deity" the less sure I am about what I mean by them anyway. It does not seem to matter. The labels are just words, and I am more interested in what actually happens.

Even prayer that is not about wanting to encounter divinity can have an impact on life. Praying routinely, socially, as meditation and so forth might not invite spiritual experiences, but this is not the only way a person can be changed. Simply having a habit of prayer changes life because it creates a space in which we *could* have a spiritual experience even if we don't particularly want to. In opening a tiny possibility, we change the shape of our lives. Even if all we do is the hurried *Dear God, please can today not be awful*, we create a moment of possibility. On its own, that moment might not amount to much. It probably won't radically change our lives and opinions. However, any kind of deliberate, ongoing practice gets us into the habit of thinking about spiritual and soulful things. It is a little bit of the day that we choose not to fill with noise, commerce, materialism or trivia. We sit down to be quiet and serious. That in turn may cause us to develop a sense of perspective, or a different attitude to life.

Taking that time may help us feel more compassion towards those around us, or more patience with ourselves. Just as a mind exercise in slowing down a bit, prayer can help us keep track of our priorities and may do something to protect us from the frequently soul-destroying culture we inhabit. No deities are required for this to work.

For people who have no desire to risk the crazy stuff, and who do not want to hear voices, prayer still has its uses. If you stick with simple and formal prayers, you can use them to just make a bit of space for being spiritual. That's well worth having even if you've no desire to develop it further. You do not have to believe anything to work this way, and no gods need to show up and bother you in person for the work to be meaningful. Just sit down with the universe for a few minutes here and there. *Hello universe. Here we all are then. Nice weather for the time of year...* It doesn't have to be epic or poetic, just whatever makes sense to you at the time.

This does seem to beg the question of why bother to pray without belief when meditation works just as well? I think there are reasons. I've studied meditation for many years, and I've written about it (*Druidry and Meditation,* Moon Books, 2012). Meditation can be used to deepen relationship, but only when we deliberately focus the meditation on something outside of ourselves. Much meditation takes us inwards, affirming that little reality bubble of one, in which we are emperors of a tiny universe. Prayer always takes us outwards because we have to address it to something. *Hello world!* may seem vague and of limited use, but it turns our attention outwards, reminding us of everything else. Used well, prayer can make us small things in a big picture, and that is good for us.

If we use meditation such that it also points us outwards, into the world, into greater awareness of that which is not us, and yet is connected to us... there's not a huge practical difference between the two disciplines. At that point the main issue is of preference. If you are a nontheist, you may feel more at ease calling the whole thing meditation – which is fine. If you are a theist of any sort, you may feel an emotional need for something you can identify as a prayer tradition. Language and concepts can be really emotive, and how we describe ourselves to ourselves, matters. Words are flimsy human attempts at quantifying everything, but limited as language is, this is what we've got with which to tell ourselves the stories of what it means to be alive. So, take the words that you can hold closely. Take the language that enables you to tell the stories that make sense. Do what you need to do and call it by those words that make it most comprehensible to you.

Chapter Twelve

Prayer and Magic

There are obvious parallels between magic and prayer. From a certain perspective, both enlist supernatural forces to try to change things in the "real" world. Petition prayers and spells can express exactly the same intentions and desires. While prayer can be framed by logic and ethics (with or without a religion to supply those) it is not a necessity. Prayer can be used to attempt to change the world in subtle and complex ways. Broader magical practice – such as undertaking ritual – can also create subtle changes. There are, as ever, things to ponder over the influence of focusing intention, and other such non-supernatural components.

As Druidry tends not to be a spell-casting tradition, magic in Druidry is more often about personal transformation than about trying to change the rest of the world. The effects of ritual and meditation may not be as clearly directed as spell work, but nonetheless have the capacity to create change. We affirm a sense of self, or a process of change, in such work. Belief is a powerful tool, which often has nothing to do with the existence or non-existence of gods.

Druids tend to understand themselves in relational ways. We exist as part of ecosystems, in webs of connections and lines of ancestry and as part of landscapes. Earth and air, wood and fire, inspiration, history and story, water and wonder... life and death weave these and so much more into the tapestry of existence. There are many shifting influences upon us, myriad forms of energy and intelligence. We are not lone sorcerers directing the flows of power and able to command the world to do our bidding. We recognise that other things have will and intention too, and as much right to self-determination as we have. We cannot set out to try to force our will upon this world. Instead we seek to engage and participate. Transformation comes through interaction, cooperation and process. Such changes are bound to be more in tune with the rest of reality, flowing or growing organically, requiring learning and adaptation. This is not the magic of the quick fix, the queue jump or the shortcut.

In Druid practice, there is inevitably a blur between prayer and magic. Both are forms of communication, ways of reaching for connection and can be expressions of relationship. While Druids do not seem to use the word "prayer" a great deal, I think a case could be made that much of Druid practice is prayer. I could equally make a case for Druidry being in essence a path of meditation and probably a bunch of other things too.

Most of the language of religion is designed for talking about actions that are identifiably different from "normal" life. The sacred and the profane underpin so much religious thinking. Druidry is different from many religions in that it does not seek to draw lines between life and spirituality, soul and earthy physicality. Therefore the standard language of religion is inadequate for expressing what we do. For Druids, the spiritual life is life. There is no separation.

Learning Druidry is a process of making your life Druidic and allowing your Druidry to permeate everything you do. It can be helpful to start this with more overt and disciplined work so that you make a point of giving time to it, until ideas and ways of being become embedded. Prayer, ritual and meditation are obvious tools to use. I find there is a constant process of blurring the edges. The attitude I learned in meditation has become very much part of my life. The quiet head-space of ritual, the reflective openness of prayer, the desire to be compassionate – I have grown into these things and they grow into me. I do not spend vast amounts of my time deliberately praying, but I am listening, more of the time than not. Whether the world speaks to me in wind, bird song or the human tongue, I am listening.

Prayer, magic, Druidry… these are human words and arbitrary divisions between things that overlap. We attempt to define and explain that which transcends language. It is an ultimately futile task, but no less important for being largely impossible. I like to talk about love, too, and I search for meaning. These are my grail quests, the impossible challenges that help to give me a sense of purpose.

Not everyone seeks total immersion in a spiritual life and not all paths function in the same way. Therefore it makes sense to also step back and consider the relationship between prayer and magic in a wider context. For the purposes of collective sanity, I'm not going to keep caveating everything, so let us assume for now that all magic and prayer have the potential to be wholly effective.

In more occult, magical practice, it is the magician who holds both responsibility and power. If you manifest your will to create change, craft a spell, or otherwise put your intent into the world, then the results are down to you. If the spell is badly made, it may backfire upon you. If you have asked for the wrong thing, you'll get that wrong thing and all the attendant consequences. Human error translates into magical failure. This encourages the spell caster to be careful and precise. Knock-on effects have to be considered, and unintended consequences must be watched for. Once you've set magic in motion, you can expect to pay for haste, error and half-baked ideas.

Petition prayer, by contrast, comes with a safety net, in most traditions. Deity is assumed to be wise and benevolent, and will check out requests before granting them. Thus anything evil, self-defeating or otherwise at odds with the divine plan, won't manifest. When a magician fails, it is their failure. When a prayer fails, it may be because the gods have other plans for you. There are some obvious psychological advantages to the prayer approach. The person whose prayers are answered doesn't have to feel too responsible for unintended side effects of what they asked for. If your benevolent god approved of the idea, clearly it's all good. This also means that when people pray for something vile, and reality delivers, their assumption of a benevolent deity in the mix can affirm a belief in their superiority and their righteousness that does no one any good at all. Belief that your prayers have been answered can be a very dangerous thing.

Not all Pagan deities are unequivocally benevolent. Many are forces of nature. Fire burns. Water drowns. Winter freezes. Death is part of nature and so are disease and decay. From a human perspective, nature is neither reliably kind, nor fair. This places most forms of Pagan prayer somewhere between magic and the prayers of many other traditions. It is not a demand in the way that magic is, but a request. The gods are at liberty to ignore us. They can also respond in ways that are not always to our liking, as we can see from reading ancient myths and, for that matter, by looking at what happens in our own lives.

Years ago, when I was young and foolish, I announced to the universe a readiness and willingness to learn. Pain, it turns out, is a very informative teacher. I feel that in the years since then, I have been shaped in very much the same way that stone sculptures are shaped; by chipping bits off. The gods do not give us what we want or think we need, that much I know. Whether what we get in life is ultimately good for us, I have no idea. None of us know who we would have been in other circumstances. All we can do is try to make the best of what we get.

Transformation is the essence of all magic, from stage tricks to the wholly serious. The nature of magic, is to beget change. On stage that often manifests as appearing and disappearing, transforming one item into another, changing the rules of physics and anatomy, or possessing apparently uncanny knowledge. Illusions of the impossible are supposed to show us that the rules of reality have been changed, just for a moment. A person can be cut in half. The magician can magically know which card you picked.

The magic of film and fiction largely postulates a reality in which stagecraft becomes real. In addition you can usually expect a bit of being able to kill people by shooting raw energy from some part of your anatomy. This is very much the magic of shortcuts: it achieves effects quickly and therefore is useful for drama and as a plot device. I doubt there's a Pagan alive who doesn't occasionally hanker after access to just that kind of magic. We all encounter miserable situations for which there are no decent, conventional solutions. Sometimes we all want an easier life, and of course there is also the inherent coolness to consider. Let's face it, the whole shooting magic out of your hands business looks good in films.

Along the way I have met people who could heal with their hands, I've met psychics and diviners. I have encountered people who can make and break atmospheres, and who know things uncannily. As yet I've not seen much in the way of magical fire, or levitation, but the part of me that will never cease to be a child, keeps looking, just in case. On reflection, I have known so many people who had small, uncanny gifts, that my perception of magic is not wholly unfounded. I've seen too many irrational things to be confident that there must be a rational explanation for everything.

Historically speaking, "magic" has meant "stuff we can't explain". Weather, luck, disease and the like have all featured heavily. Most of our modern technology would seem like magic from the perspective of our ancestors. We still struggle to explain why one particular child gets leukaemia or why one family is wiped out in a car crash. We all experience random events that have no more rational explanation than "shit happens". When you look at them closely, the building blocks of our lives are improbable events balancing on previous unlikely outcomes, underpinned by million-to-one chances. When you think about the odds it took for all your ancestors to survive, meet and breed successfully, even being here in the first place seems to defy the odds. Most of the planets we know about don't even have the conditions to generate life in the first place. From a rational perspective, there's nothing supernatural occurring in any of this. On the other hand, part of the idea of magic, for some people, is that you don't do anything supernatural there, either. You just get into the flow of all that random improbability and direct it a bit so that things work out in the manner of your choosing. The trouble with doing this kind of magic is that you can't prove things wouldn't have worked out that way without it.

So, let's turn the whole thing on its head. Magic is change. Therefore we might also say, change is magic (with a nod to Alice, who felt that "I say what I mean" and "I mean what I say" were interchangeable statements). We live in a world where cause and effect are the known mechanics of change. One thing causes another. This can suggest a mechanical inevitability in everything that happens to us. As that's a dull way of looking at life, I'm not going to bother to dwell upon it further. In practice, that flow from cause to effect is only a clear process in retrospect. Most causes create many possible outcomes, and sometimes it is not the most likely probabilities that manifest as the given effect. What breaks one person makes another more determined, and ultimately more successful. In the realms of human thought and emotion, cause and effect is a complicated business. How we think about the causes has a great deal of impact on the effects.

Druidry tends not to favour spell-based magic. We are more likely to seek magical transformation through the experience of ritual, prayer, meditation and all the rest of life. In such work, we aren't trying to force changes onto external reality, but instead seek to foster change inside ourselves. Get a magical fix for a problem and you aren't going to be equipped for the next fairly similar one that comes along. We learn and grow by being challenged. It is also worth bearing in mind that most of life is not made up of dramatic, life-or-death scenarios for which no ordinary solution exists. Most of life consists of smaller, passably predictable challenges and setbacks. We learn to navigate through existence by tackling these until they become easy for us. As babies, we could not feed ourselves, control our bowels or get about. Most of us are able to learn to do those things and all the other small but important things that come along as well.

The challenges that give us a really hard time, are the ones we are least psychologically equipped to deal with. The person who has always been a high achiever can be broken by the first failed exam. A laid-back person may find a messy toddler easy to deal with, while someone who is compulsively tidy may be infuriated and made miserable by the same experience. A person crippled by anxiety can be overwhelmed in situations that healthier people would not consider stressful. Managing the ordinary business of life is only difficult when we are dealing with our own limitations and shortcomings.

Magical transformations can be all about dealing with personal shortcomings. Learning to overcome the aspects of self that we find inhibiting is an on-going struggle, but a productive one. Our beliefs, desires and attitudes can all be part of what restricts us, or part of what liberates us. Liberation, in turn, can seem like a daunting prospect for some. It may feel safer to remain stuck inside our excuses. *I'm not good enough. I'm not clever enough to do that. It'll go wrong. People like me never...* Finding the courage to challenge our own assumptions can be the biggest transformative experience of them all.

This kind of transformation, occurring inside the self, is no more supernaturally magical than is the internet or an airplane. All that happens when we change ourselves, is that we start a process of learning, experimenting, assessing and rethinking. Some bits of that process may happen unconsciously, below the radar of the one making the transition. Our not noticing a shift does not make it an entirely inexplicable psychological event though, it just means we don't spot it at the time. Even so, when the results of inner change become visible to us, they can be as surprising as the rabbit out of the hat is to someone who'd never seen that before. The more familiar we are with something, the less likely we are to see it as magical, because we'll have growing suspicions about how it really works. The rabbit out of the hat gets less impressive at each repetition. We know what the flourished hat means, and we have a good idea where he's stuck the rabbit... Even if we can't see them, we can reason them out, and so it is with the unseen functions of ourselves. You might not see how meditation makes you calmer, but once you've matched the cause to the effect a few times, you'll be fairly sure of what you're dealing with. That which we can understand or think we know, can be taken for granted and becomes mundane to us. That, however, is not necessarily a good development. All change is magic. Hold that thought. A little enchantment with the allegedly mundane is a good thing.

Part of the process of magic in Druidry is one of re-enchantment. This is the work of re-learning in which we rediscover the world. Everything around us is not just a series of backdrops for the movie of your life. Other people are not bit-parts and extras. Every living thing is just as alive as we are. Every material thing is just as tangible as we are. Everything we encounter has its own story and history, its own place in the world. Each blade of grass is unique, and every last one is precious.

A person does not go round seeing the world they inhabit as so much props and set design, and then wake up into a full awareness of the enormity of life. That would be insanity inducing. Re-enchantment is a process. We start wherever we need to. Perhaps that means learning to see other humans as unique, precious and autonomous individuals. Too many humans seem to struggle with that one. From there, we might progress to learning to see creatures, plants and all the other living wonders of this world as being valuable too; each miracle of existence a treasure to inspire and enchant us.

Re-enchantment imbues all life with meaning. It gives us a very different kind of perspective and value system. Rather than having the make-believe movie in our heads, re-enchantment takes us into the present, and into the real world. We stop giving ourselves total supremacy in all things, and learn how to fall in love with everything around us.

Prayer can be thoroughly at odds with re-enchantment. If we are using prayer to try to transcend the material world, we are feeding our disenchantment. If we pray to reinforce our sense of specialness, such that we think we are the beloved of God, the main protagonist in the great epic of our lives, we stay disenchanted. Prayer is simply a tool. How we use it informs the outcome. Cause and effect manifest again, with all the same caveats about never quite knowing how things will turn out or what, precisely, made the difference. Sometimes, despite our best efforts, life conspires to re-enchant us anyway. Anything we do that gives us empathy or insight, has the potential to show us the wonder of existence, and that experience in turn will change us.

If we pray to learn, that can assist us in the process of re-enchantment. It doesn't really matter who or what we pray to. The important thing in this context is being open to, and aware of, something beyond us. We break down the privacy of the world inside our skulls, a little. Something else is then able to get in. Not something occult, or unreal, but the actual existence of things beyond us. We might then learn to empathise with that which is not us, and start to care about it. I suspect most Druids will already be some way into this process, but on the whole, western minds are focused on utility. If we cannot make use of something, we view it as irrelevant. We do that to ourselves, and to each other as well. What is the point of wasps? As though their utility defines their right to exist. We see resources and opportunities where we need to see other aware and living beings. Re-enchantment teaches us to love things simply because they are there. We learn to appreciate, to see beauty. We might even get less interested in looking for economic applications. Not all worth can be measured with money.

When it comes to making slow changes in the mind that can strike us as being magical, prayer is a usable tool. Just the act of praying can cause some of those mind magic mysteries. As before observed, our failure to notice or understand a process does not make it any less real or useful. Science-based Cognitive Behavioural Therapy relies on getting us to make changes that we don't always see happening. Just by repeatedly doing things or thinking in slightly different language, significant psychological problems can be overcome. With prayer and meditation alike, we can chip away at the unpleasantly hard edges we use to define ourselves.

The modern, western world is all about those hard, self-defensive edges. Walls around property and walls around our things, ideally with alarms on. Ownership and demarcation are important to us. We need to see those physical boundaries. We associate immobility and inflexibility with strength and virtue. Under certain circumstances, rigid strength will turn out to be brittle. That which cannot change, cannot adapt. If we pray to make ourselves open, rather than to reinforce our own prejudices, prayer softens us. It erodes both the walls in our minds and the desire for walls. We can choose to undertake the process in order to make ourselves more empathic, softer, more yielding and more open. This can be uncomfortable, but brings its own rewards, too. If we become less rigid, we can feel excited, impressed, or enchanted. These are good sensations. Happiness is not a product of walls, and the most rigid people are often also the most miserable ones, in my experience.

The magic of change and the power of evolving deserve embracing in their own right. These are things to want for their own sake, not just in anticipation of where they might take us. Learning not to cling too hard to certainty (which is never as certain as we want it to be). Learning not to draw lines between ourselves and our fears. Learning to live, wide-eyed and wondering. We do not have to shut ourselves in like battery hens, walled up by our fears of freedom and the responsibility it brings. We do not have to buy into the lie that caring is too difficult and painful. If you are free, there is no room for excuses, no fobbing yourself off with lame justifications for not living. If you are responsible, you have to deal with the consequence of what you do. That also means giving yourself the power to step up to those consequences. The magic of change is certainly no kind of shortcut.

One of the effects of inner transformation is that it can then change our attitudes to aspects of our lives. In practice it is often easier to change our minds than our circumstances. Changing how we think can also be a way of tackling otherwise intractable difficulties. How we think informs how we understand what we experience. It is easy to inflate and distort experience with faulty thinking. Where we bring personal baggage, error or assumptions to a problem, we can easily worsen it. Expecting the past to repeat in the future can underpin anxiety, while believing we can do the same things and get different results, can underpin psychosis.

Our expectations inform how we interpret our life experiences. Often we find what we were looking for, which can distort our understanding. Just trying to look for something different can radically change our experiences. Holding the belief that life should be fairer, better, easier or otherwise different can cause a great deal of pain. Sometimes the best way to cope with life is simply being able to accept it, warts and all. The perspective of some religions; that the hard bits should be understood as "part of God's mysterious plan" can be one way of coming to terms with this. Most Druids are not monotheists, however. As soon as you consider multiple manifestations of deity, animism or atheism as perspectives, scope for "God's mysterious plan" reduces. There are simply too many intelligences out there to suggest the existence of one grand plan, as I see things. However, it's also worth noting that in polytheist mythologies, gods go round attempting to thwart each other, so of course being beloved of one deity isn't any guarantee of ease, and may attract the bad feelings of other deities. Atheist thinking precludes divine plans for obvious reasons, but also offers no reason to assume life should be other than it is, which works perfectly well too. It's only when we imagine that belief should translate into worldly advantage, or that we are entitled to something we don't have, that the problems start.

The Reformed, and Newly Reformed Druids of North America have an interesting approach to this: nature is good. It's a very challenging concept. Death, violence, suffering, disease and decay are all necessary parts of nature. It can be more comfortable to view nature as morally neutral. The statement "nature is good" is an acceptance that life includes all of the bits we don't like. These are not optional things, nor irritations we should be able to get rid of. Life depends on death. Growth depends upon decay. The blood, mess and visceral gore of existence are also intrinsic to existence. Nature is good.

Acceptance does not have to mean apathy or inaction. It does, however, make the challenges of life easier to bear. This is not the easiest path to walk, either. Nothing is entirely easy. It has taken me a long time to accept that sometimes, there is no justice. My childhood desire for fairness, so heavily reinforced by fairy stories, has taken a lot of getting to grips with. Poetic justice is in woefully short supply much of the time. I have been through a process, alongside the research for and creation of this book, where I've had to deal with profound injustice. It's entered my life in a number of different ways, frustrating, depressing, and sometimes maddening. I have come to realise that if I want justice and other things of that ilk to exist, I have to put them into the world. If I want peace, I have to act in ways that promote, cause and enable peace. Shouting about its absence isn't going to help. I have to do the work.

Without first accepting how things actually are, it is very difficult to formulate change. Acceptance requires a knowledge of truth. That too can be hard to achieve. Truth can be a painful, unpredictable thing. It can be easier to pretend there is no problem, and to cling to our illusions. Very little good comes out of that, only the most illusory, fragile kind of short-term peace, often bought at a very high price. When we ignore the truth, we tend to make things worse for ourselves, and others. I write from a place of grim experience on this subject. In the past I have refused to recognise that some people's words and actions were incredibly toxic for me. I stayed in pain because of that, limited, damaged and unable to do the best that I could. In addition, through my refusal to see what was happening, I caused suffering to those around me who could have done with my being more functional. When I eventually accepted the unwelcome truth, I became able to act and made the necessary changes.

It is my belief that acceptance does not mean giving up on dreams or relinquishing action. Acceptance is a solid foundation from which you can build productively. I did not set out deliberately to walk this path. I prayed to be able to manifest peace, harmony and goodness in the world. What this has taught me, slowly over a period of many months, is the importance of acceptance. I expect less of life than I did, although I am blessed with a happier existence than I have ever known before. I accept those things I cannot fix, and through that am able to make more functional and realistic choices. I am working to accept my own limitations, and to therefore do a better job of working within them.

By undertaking to pray, I created a causal situation from which I wanted certain effects. In practice, I did not appreciate the many steps necessary to go from where I was, to where I want to be. That process is happening anyway, and I have no idea where that will take me, but it's fine.

In recent weeks, I've found the strength to take the fight to an organisation that has plagued me for years with its unjust and unreasonable behaviour. I've written most of this book while living on a narrowboat, at the mercy of The Canal & River Trust. This is a "charity" that, at the time of writing, uses money raised from public donation to fund an enforcement department. That department routinely threatens to make homeless, people who live on their boats. It is an obscene system and an affront to the very idea of charity, as I see it. Every time I accepted its actions, I effectively allowed it to continue. Every time I felt too powerless to challenge what seems to me like bullying behaviour, there was no justice. I've grown braver in the past year, and more able to trust my own judgment. I am not asking anything supernatural to win this fight for me. I just want the means to bring about justice. *Give me the tools, and I will use them.* I'm not waiting for help to come, I'm signing petitions, writing letters, and I've become actively involved in local politics. I do what I can to support harassed boaters, to raise awareness of this ongoing injustice, and to make change. Through reducing my fear of punishment I have become more able to resist bullies.

That said, I'd have no aversion to a bit of poetic justice and some divine intervention. The absence of dependable evidence for either, does not take away the desire to see them manifest. There are times when the impulse to pray and the desire to curse are one and the same. The longing for deity turns into something a bit like wanting the power to even the odds. The promise of something to offset your poverty and material powerlessness has always been an attractive aspect of religions. From our ancient Pagan ancestors trying to placate the gods into giving them a decent harvest, to the most modern of enemy-smiting impulses, magic and prayer alike often come down to little more than a desire not to be heading to hell in a bucket of snot this time.

Dear anything at all, give me a break. Give me a chance, let it go my way this time. Sometimes it does, sometimes it doesn't, and we'll see the evidence for and against supernatural influence according to our inclinations.

Chapter Thirteen

Making Druid Prayers

If we are going to pray, then we need our own prayers. No matter what we believe or intend, the prayers we offer need to resonate with us and make emotional sense. The language and style of our prayers, the tone and the underpinning concepts need to come from the fabric of our beliefs and other practices. Inevitably this is highly individual. That said, a lot of modern Druidry is very wordy. Our rituals are full of words. We talk and debate whenever a few Druids gather together. We tell stories and make poems. Ancient Druidry was an oral tradition, with a vast array of words to commit to memory. While those historic words are lost to us, the hunger for linguistic expression remains. We might go out to dance with the wind, singing the wordless songs of soil, tree and ancestry, but we'll come back and talk about it afterwards.

There is a magic in language, and a real power. The tricks and nuances of words enable us to affect each other's feelings, to craft atmospheres and share inspiration. Equally, words can subvert and mislead, for good or ill. If I tell you "Thou Shalt", we're in a whole other place from if I say "you will" while "you could" is yet a whole other thing again. As Druids, we bring language to that which defies language. We attempt to speak that which cannot be spoken.

There is no one right way of using words, nor are there specific "right words" to use. However, we could start by considering that every use of words can be understood as a prayer or a spell. Every word expresses intention, and relationship. Each word we deploy is a manifestation of our Druidry. To speak or write carelessly, with no eye to possible misunderstandings, potential offence, no thought for nuances or undertones, is to fail in this regard. Of course we all fail. In weariness and ill health, in confusion and frustration, we all muff up. I have no idea if it is possible to get into a state of speaking from a place of conscious Druidry all the time. I do know that it's worth trying for. With that in mind, this chapter will, in part, be an exploration of the language of prayer.

Improvisation

Prayers of petition and gratitude tend to happen in the moment, coming as a direct response to life. As a consequence, both are more likely to be improvised than planned. Nonetheless, we will deploy our terms of preference as we direct the prayer.

Thank you Earth, for this moment, this balmy sun and the peace of this place.

Dear God, make it stop!

If you don't have any definite focus to which prayers can be directed, an expressed sense of gratitude is no less real or valuable. Pleas for help seem equally likely to be unanswered whether you have a deity in mind or not. What is useful, is that we acknowledge our feelings and let them out. This kind of improvised prayer can be the expression of last resort, more useful as catharsis than anything else. "If all else fails, we might get some relief from shouting, "All the gods are bastards!" There may be a place for prayers of ingratitude on the improvising list, as well. Whether we "should" or not, we all get moments of wanting to, or actually, berating deity for letting us down or protesting that the gods joke at our expense. Perhaps they do. All the ancient tales I've read suggest that there is no reason to assume deities are always kindly. "As flies to wanton boys are we to the Gods, they kill us for their sport", as Shakespeare says in *King Lear,* and Thomas Hardy recycled for *Tess of the D'Urbervilles.* If we suspect deity of acting this way, prayers of ingratitude might at least help us hang onto some dignity.

No, gods, I did not deserve this, and no, I am not beaten, and no, I did not appreciate the educational angle of that recent experience.

In improvised prayer, speaking in the moment we will most likely use habitual language. The words we normally employ are the ones most readily available to us. When we aren't preparing our words in advance, we will pay least attention to the undertones and the quality of our expression. This can make it an interesting measure of what we have absorbed. The Druid who unconsciously invokes "Jesus Christ!" in moments of frustration has probably not internalised a Celtic worldview yet, or is still significantly influenced by their background. The more ritual form we have experienced, the more likelihood there is of our improvisations taking a ritual tone. The authors we read, friends we listen to, and mentors who guide us may shape our speech.

While rituals can be formulaic and scripted, there are groups who favour improvisation – often within a pre-agreed framework. In such rituals, calling to the ancestors, elementals, spirits of place or whoever else you honour, can be a form of prayer. These can be times to ask for presence, for blessings, for the rain to hold off... A more improvised approach makes it possible to say what makes sense in the moment. Given the influence of climate when working outside, this can be an important consideration. While improvising can be more rough and ready, it will always be relevant, and that can be worth the trade off against planning and poetry. The most beautiful words in honour of the sun will sound odd if the sun is notably obscured.

There are times when improvisation can become a magical experience in its own right. When a Druid enters the flow of awen, spontaneous poetic speech is possible. Exquisite language, full of depth and significance can be the product of an inspired moment. It might seem more realistic to seek such inspiration quietly, at the writing table, where failure is not public, but for those who dare, poetry can be sought in ritual.

My most memorable experience of flowing inspiration came

when a group of musicians spontaneously made music in ritual. With no plan, and no conversation, a piece of music came together out of nowhere. When the awen flows in this way, a prayer made in the moment can be an incredibly intense and magical experience. There's a sense that the energy of it passes through you, coming from somewhere else and journeying on into the world. Regardless of the context, this kind of prayer does not feel like a one-sided monologue. Some kind of dialogue is happening, which the Druid is able to express in the moment. In my experience, the more time an individual gives to improvised work, the more possible these moments of ecstatic inspiration become.

In truly inspired improvisation, it can be hard to decide whether the prayer even comes from the person who voices it. Awen infused moments can leave a person more inclined to feel that something has happened to them, than that they have created a thing. Prayer may come as a response to vision and insight, to a sense of presence or that feeling the universe is speaking through you. Prayer may be directed to others in the ritual, to uplift and inspire them into action. It may be spoken on behalf of the community. This is a very different experience to any one-sided speeches that do not result in a sense of connection and also from prayers that come from the individual and seem to connect them to the wider world. When the awen flows, prayer becomes an expression of spiritual experience, rather than an attempt to induce one.

Writing

The written prayer is a much more self-conscious and considered creation. That in itself can encourage a more formal approach. There's a more permanent feel to a written prayer, too; a sense that you might be leaving something for posterity or creating something that might pass into other hands. As a consequence there is both time and reason to carefully create a thing of beauty.

A written prayer is more likely to be something it might be worth saying to the divine, rather than a flashed response to crisis and need. Presenting this kind of work to a human audience can be intimidating enough. Trying to craft words worthy of offering to deity is even more so. The improvised approach to prayer can be easier simply because it does not offer us too much time in which to consider the implications. It is also worth bearing in mind that a written prayer suggests the possibility of a human audience. Unlike deities, humans tend to give direct feedback.

I have encountered Pagans online mentioning the way in which deity has worked with them to enable them to write prayers or liturgy. My own feelings about this, is that it's a bit like getting your teacher to do your homework. If you have the kind of deity that wants you to say or do things they will find pleasing, this might make sense. If your relationship with the divine is more like a dialogue, then bringing your own ideas to your half of it makes a lot of sense. If all we can say to the gods is that which we think the gods have told us to say, I'm not sure what the point is. A parent or teacher analogy suggests this is quite a problematic approach. It comes back to our reasons for seeking the divine, whether we think the point of life is to submit to divinity, or we see gods as beings to work with in harmonious ways.

When it comes to writing prayers, the first consideration is length. The longer a prayer is, the harder it will be to learn and the greater the risk that humans (and non-humans) listening, will grow bored. There is little scope for a spiritual experience when people are tapping their feet and eyeing their watches. It is not the job of a single prayer to try to convey everything you have ever wanted to express to the divine.

Here I think it pays to take a sideways glance at magical practice: good spells are often simple, or at least very clear in their intent. A prayer, like a spell, is a focusing of your intention, emotion or belief. While in prayer you may not be shooting for a specific outcome, the focus still matters. Aiming to create a short prayer can be an excellent way of keeping the endeavour precise and punchy. That doesn't mean envisaging a 140-character tweet to God, but it does suggest avoiding something akin to an essay. Less is often more, and the process of refining what you want to say down to something simple and clear, is well worth the effort.

Like stories, prayers have a beginning, a middle and an end. It is well worth considering how they function. The beginning of the prayer is our address to the divine. In that opening part, we have to consider what we call them/it and what words we frame that with. If you have a specific, named deity in mind, that part is fairly simple. Be it Freya, Artemis or Bast, if you have a person-ified deity, you know who you are trying to talk to and that name acts as an excellent focus. The next easiest are those where your idea is clear even if a name is missing – seeking the spirit of the wood you stand in, or the patron deity of an activity, or virtue. It is easy to work up an address around such concepts.

You who watch over this land.

You who my ancestors worshipped in this place.

You who are in the bean and inspire the mysterious delights of chocolate.

In such cases, with spirits named or unnamed, we might also want to include titles. Some methods of addressing deity are all about authority: Lord of the greenwood, Master of the forge, Queen of the night, Lady of the healing waters. It's hard to imagine using other authority titles, Chairman of the dancing flames, Major of the wheeling stars. Baron of the flourishing herbs. We tend towards words that suggest ultimate power, and undemocratic power at that. Deity seems more conducive to the language of feudalism than democracy. Perhaps that's part of why religion winds up so many rational atheists.

Oh duly elected spirits who preside over this place. Oh Prime Minister of the Gods.

It doesn't work.

If our relationship with deity is less power-orientated in the first place, however, those titles soon become irrelevant. Words that honour and show respect may seem more appropriate. *Oh noble spirit of the ancient oak. Oh dancing spirit of the glad hearth fire,* and so forth.

For those who cast themselves in a more familial relationship with deity, Mother and Father are often titles of preference. We can take that language into less humanoid connections, too. Why not Grandfather Mountain and Grandmother Forest? Such words are an invitation to think more widely about who our brothers and sisters are in such a context. Who shares our parents and grandparents of spirit? Who should we consider to be our equals?

Alternatively, we can consider the language of adoration and admiration. *Beloved. Honoured, Oh Great and Mighty...* This one raises some interesting questions, too. Most importantly, what are we aiming to achieve here? Are we addressing the divine in a way that expresses relationship, or are we trying to butter them up? As Druids, it really should be the former, not the latter. The kinds of gods who need grovelling, obsequious humans to sing their praises are nothing but trouble.

Any of these modes of address can be put together, and so we can say...

Beloved Lady of the forest, you who walk in sunlight and in shadow, holding the deep mysteries of the land. Grandmother of us all, Queen of the fertile soil and the abundant trees...

While this sort of language can feel like overkill for those who tend towards plainer speaking, it does have its uses. The point of the address is to focus your mind on the deity you wish to connect with, commune with or otherwise bother. Pagans of a more Reconstructionist persuasion back this up by using whatever rituals, items and correspondences they feel will be pleasing to, and likely to get the attention of, the deity in question, based on historical research. This is also worth a thought. We may think about the divine at times when we aren't seeking its attention. Being able to flag up that right now, we really would like to communicate, can be very productive. A little formality can help to define whether we were serious or not.

If you bother the same deity on a regular basis, have a feeling of relationship and are confident about not drawing their attention by accident, then *Hello my Lady, me again...* might be all you feel you need. If the idea of reaching out to deity is challenging, then the more involved evocation can be a way of talking yourself into the right sort of headspace. That stream of descriptive words can help focus the mind, and through that can facilitate a sense of connection. There is an art to finding what works, and like all art forms, it takes practise. Don't expect to get things right all the time, and certainly don't expect dramatic results when you start. All aspects of spirituality are like learning a skill or craft. We don't expect to pick up an instrument one day and play concerts the next. We need to be patient with our spiritual lives and resist expectations of instant results. Talking to deity might be likened to talking in a foreign language, one with a different alphabet, unfamiliar grammar rules and mysterious underlying concepts. If we were learning a foreign language, we would assume it might take a while to be able to manage a conversation.

The middle section of your prayer is the bit where you explain why you wanted the deity's attention. That might be a petition, to express gratitude, to seek awareness of them and ask what they would have you do. Clearly expressing your intention is important, not least because it keeps you focused on what you're trying to achieve. Even if you don't manage anything else, that focus helps you develop qualities within yourself, as previously discussed. I think the hardest thing to do in prayer is to sit in true silence and listen. The mind wanders. Even a passably disciplined mind will process background noise, think about a desired outcome, wonder if that thought was somehow a divine sanction after all, and generally tie itself in knots thereafter. Repeating a simple prayer formula can be more productive. It is worth exploring a mix of repetition and mental silence, using word-prayers as a way to hold those silences when you can, making them more viable by refocusing as needed. This is a good way of putting a wandering mind back on the intended track.

There are language considerations around the middle section of prayer, too. What is the etiquette of speaking to deity? Are we using a language of self-abasement, *unworthy servant, lowly sinner* and all that? Are we asking the gods to feel sorry for us? Have we thought about the kinds of gods they are, and considered how unlikely that approach is to work? Are we trying the *please can I have, I promise I'll be really good* style of the child asking a parent for a puppy? How we phrase our requests and approaches reflects what we imagine the relationship to be between ourselves and the divine. That could have an impact on the outcomes, not least because it will influence our own thinking. If every prayer says *sorry gods, I'm totally useless, worthless and made of fail, and only your greatness can save me,* then we are reinforcing some horrendously negative self-images. Alternatively, *Father, lend me your power so that I can kill our enemies* is going to leave some nasty marks on your mind as well.

We pray from a basis of who we are and, at the same time, the language of our prayers will shape the people we are becoming. I cannot stress enough the importance of paying attention to what words mean, both at the surface use, and in undertones and connotations. Imprecise language use causes pain, confusion, mistakes and anger. What we learn to get right in prayer, we might manage to handle better in the rest of our lives, too.

Dear gods, please stop sending me professional people who do not understand the meanings of the words they deploy, and whose ability to reimagine the meanings of my words is creative to the point of inducing insanity. Please, at least, can I have some professional people who are capable of continuity in their language deployment. That would make a nice change.

The third part of prayer, is how we end it. Do we say, *Thanks, bye!* As though hanging up the holy telephone? The Christians have this neatly resolved with "Amen" as the religious alternative to over-and-out. I have heard Druids tagging "Awen" onto the end of prayers in the same way. I don't think it works. The sonorous similarity between amen and awen draws in energy that feel out of place in a Druid context. It also feels a lot like the rather lazy theft of someone else's traditions. Wiccans use the phrase "So may/mote it be" to round up all manner of things. Sometimes borrowing this for Druidry can work, especially where a human intention or dedication is being expressed.

We shall plant a hundred trees. So may it be.

In other forms of prayer, a "So may it be" is a bit like making a demand, which isn't terribly Druidic either. That leaves us with no formal, tidy ending, which is excellent news. In the absence of neat solutions handed down from on high, only individual approaches remain.

There is something about prayer that suggests the need for a formal rounding off. That may in part be due to monotheistic influences. I do feel though that if you have just tried to get the attention of a deity, then closing that down afterwards calls for some art and intention too. Some expression of gratitude seems appropriate, and deliberate words of stepping away also help us reconnect with the world. Again, what seems most important here is being able to manage our own minds and intentions. If we do not have that in hand, do we really imagine we can work with the divine? We make a point of carefully ending rituals, and we need to take the same approach with prayer. Leaving the prayer headspace in a deliberate way, is important. There are issues of respect for both self and deity here. It's a bit like departing from someone's house – even if they aren't there, you must still leave respectfully and you do leave, because it is not your space. When we pray, we are visiting, and there comes a time to return from whence we came.

Voicing Prayer

Prayer can of course be silent. A lot of the time, silence is necessary if you want any kind of privacy. If you work outside of a recognised prayer space, anyone encountering you may find your praying weird, and may respond to it in unhelpful ways. Private, silent prayer is a safe enough process, socially speaking. Voicing prayer is a whole other issue.

Vocal prayer can be quite aggressive or offensive if undertaken in the company of people who do not wish to participate. Religions can be a lot like sex in that regard, with the same degree of careful sounding out required before anything actually happens. If the situation would not be a suitable one for exposing your genitals without checking first, it probably isn't suitable for exposing your faith, either. Only if those present are comfortable with what you intend to do, and give informed consent, is sharing prayer with others appropriate. As an aside, the whole exposed genitals parallel does not, by extension, identify swingers' parties or nudist beaches as good places to pray!

Speaking prayer aloud, even in a whisper, is very different from the silent, in the head stuff. This is an act of putting something into the world. Speech is usually slower than thought, leaving us time as we voice the words in which to dwell upon the meaning and intent. If we have a human audience, the words we intone may have an effect on them, too. Spoken prayers can move and inspire the people who hear them. If we get it wrong, our prayers can be an active turn-off, a topic I'll come back to in the next chapter.

Our voices are the single most important ritual tool in Druidry. The voice is not so vital in solitary work, but if you are out with a group, it is vocal work that shapes a ritual and how we use our voices has great influence on atmosphere. I have never worked in ritual with someone who could not speak or hear, although I have worked with people who were impaired. It may be that Druidry, with its roots in oral tradition, might not hold much appeal for someone totally vocally or aurally disabled. However, if that is your situation or you encounter someone dealing with it, bear this in mind: there is no one true way. Just because I prioritise the voice does not mean Druidry cannot be expressed by other means. All traditions exist because people created them. If current norms, or my suggestions, do not suit your needs, then it falls to you to innovate and create what you need. It is always fine to do this. In fact, I would argue that creativity and innovation are more innately Druidic than just rehashing what's already out there.

As things stand at the moment, speech is the primary conveyor of ritual content and most rituals are made largely from words. Prayers tend to be made of words as well.

The voice is an incredibly powerful, intimate thing. We can identify individuals by their voices alone if we have heard them speak a few times. Voices tend to reveal our genders, suggest our ages, and can often convey other details about our social backgrounds. In speech we can reveal our emotions, or create an impression of other sentiments in order to play a part. Depending on our skills and intentions, speech can be a natural representation of self, or wholly contrived to create an impression. There is a further consideration in that emoting with the voice can create emotion within us. Voice and emotion are very much linked. If we make a point of speaking reverently, we will incline ourselves to feel more reverence, and so forth.

The first consideration, if we have decided to pray out loud, is volume. This will be dictated to a fair degree by the situation. Vocalising in a place that is quiet, but not private, may lend itself to muted tones or whispers. When offering prayer to a ritual circle or in a larger, designated, space the projection skills of the theatre are very much called for. If you have a human audience, they need to be able to hear you. In some cases, that may even call for amplification. Paying attention to the acoustics of a place can help get your voice to carry.

Clarity is essential. It is much easier to speak clearly when you know what you want to say. Reading unfamiliar words off a sheet seldom makes for clear and flowing speech. If you create short and focused prayers in the first place, then committing them to memory is a good deal easier. Improvised prayers need to be well articulated too. If you aren't confident about improvising or remembering, then the sheet of paper is a better bet than minutes of ums and uncomfortable pauses. Losing your way is not conducive to making a connection, nor is feeling anxiety or self-consciousness. Holding a piece of paper can be a barrier to prayer – focused on reading, we may not be thinking about the meaning at all. Whatever gives you most scope for clarity and communication is the right answer. Give yourself room for what you do to change with practise, as well.

Unless you engage with the meaning of the prayer, it is just so many words. As you speak, there needs to be a process of thinking and feeling the meaning. If you can invest the prayer with your feelings, that helps. From a prayer-before-audience perspective, this can create drama and interest. However, it is important not to let the desire for drama take over from actual content. Whatever you need to say, should be voiced sincerely. Fake emotion for the sake of dramatic effect, is not good Druidry.

Attention can also be paid to pacing. Often for public speech it pays to slow down. Nerves can cause us to accelerate our words, and deliberately reducing the pace helps combat this. Slower words are easier to comprehend, and also carry better in a large space. There is a gravitas to slower speech, which reinforces a sense of ceremony and significance. The use of small silences allows time to draw breath and reflect. Silence, used well, adds depth and poignancy.

It is important to breathe. For those not used to speaking

publically, this is often an issue. Running out of breath mid phrase can destroy the flow and sense of a sentence. Nerves can leave us short of breath, while projection requires a good flow of air. Avoid writing large sentences in the first place if you can. Get to know the patterns of your own phrasing and breathing when you speak naturally. Working with your natural rhythms is always the most effective approach. Practise reading out loud to get a sense of what is easy for you, and what you struggle with. Any texts will do. When you practise words or songs destined for public airing, also practise breathing. Work out when you need to draw breath. This will improve both your confidence and your performance.

The tone of voice you employ can support, or undermine, your language. If you are planning an angry rant against the gods, or humanity, don't delivery it meekly. If you mean to petition for something, try not to sound too smug. Whining and self-pity are not going to help you. Consider your relationship with deity and speak honestly from there, as best you can. Again, don't let the desire to be ritually theatrical get between you and the meaning. A bombastic voice may carry well, but it won't convey much emotional range. If in doubt, remember that ritual is a means, and not an end in itself.

What Shall We Pray For?

There are certain kinds of prayer that make particular sense in a Druid context. This isn't an exhaustive list, just the things that seemed most obvious to me. Life will throw up specific situations that may suggest specific prayers, which I cannot hope to cover here. These are broad approaches, generally applicable.

Gratitude. We all have much to be grateful for, starting from the fact of our existence and expanding out to every part of our lives. That which hurts and challenges us can also help us grow. All of it; the good and the bad, makes up the sum of our experience. These are the things that shape us. This is what our lives are made of. We can go beyond that, looking for what seems especially good, beautiful or precious. Expressing gratitude for the good stuff cultivates an attitude very much in tune with modern Druidry. Seeing the good, responding to it, praising, appreciating and supporting, all help to make life that bit better for ourselves and for others.

Strength and courage. For me this one represents half of the productive side of petition prayer. If the solutions are given to me, I do not learn or grow. Experience to date suggests that petitioning for an easy way out seldom works anyway. However, asking for the strength to endure, and the means to do the necessary work, is not about getting off lightly. It is about developing a quality of self. Christine Hoff Kraemer identifies developing personal virtue as the essence of Pagan ethics,[23] so anything that helps there, is probably good.

Often I find it's the case that I know what the solution is, but I am afraid to take the necessary action. Fear of failure or of looking like an ass. Fear of making things worse. Fear that I have misunderstood, or that my solution is faulty. So often this is where I falter when faced with a challenge. What I need is not freedom from fear. Those fears are useful; they stop me from being complacent and overconfident. What I need is courage, to know when to trust myself and jump. In asking for strength and courage, we are asking for the means to do the work before us. Whether deity responds or not, time spent thinking about these virtues can help us through the crisis, or psyche us up to make the necessary leap into the unknown.

The second kind of petition I think is wholly consistent with Druidry, is the petition for inspiration. We may pray to deity, or to the flow of awen. Again, this is not a petition to get out of something. Inspiration solves problems, but does not take them away. Inspiration reduces insurmountable obstacles to hills we can feasibly climb. Inspiration allows us to look properly at the rock and the hard place, and respond by growing some wings.

We do not even have to ask that the spark of insight comes to us from outside. It can just be about creating the right mental conditions to find our own way through. Again, the process of asking can lead us in the right direction without any external input.

Relationship. The idea of all things existing in relationship is intrinsic to Druidry. Therefore I think a fourth inherently Druidic approach to prayer, is to use it as a way of seeking connection. We can pray to reach out, from a desire to experience, understand, learn and be changed by what we encounter.

I spent a lot of time wondering if healing should be on this list, as well. I think there are two ways of considering whether we should pray for healing. On one hand, healing is good; saving lives, eliminating pain and arguably we should pray for healing as an act of compassion towards ourselves and others. On the other hand, death is part of nature, and inevitable. Pain can bring our greatest life lessons. There are wholly Druidic arguments both for and against praying for healing, just as there are around praying for peace. Sometimes, peace and healing are exactly what is called for. Sometimes, an entirely different thing needs to happen before those outcomes would be realistic and sustainable anyway. Do whatever makes sense. Again, prayers that seek to find a good way through may be more effective than those that assume we know what the best method or outcome would actually be. Sometimes the most useful thing to do is seek insight, not solutions.

Beyond this list of more general prayer types, we may also want to consider dedications. There are moments in life when we make momentous decisions about how to proceed. Marriage and parenting are often marked by rites of passage, but there are many others. Commitments to study, to serve, to greener living, peace, activism and more can be the basis for dedications made as part of our Druidry. Offering such dedications in ritual can have a powerful effect, binding us to the chosen course. Dedications give us human witnesses, who can support and encourage us. What we swear to do, in prayer and dedication, can be very binding indeed, so it needs to be well considered and carefully worded. Heat of the moment declarations that you will serve a named deity with every last breath in your body, love someone forever, or never eat an animal product, can have unintended consequences. Reality, I have noticed, can have a slightly twisted sense of humour sometimes.

Making a dedication is like binding a spell of intent around your actions. Doing so takes ideas out of the realm of daydream and helps them solidify. The formality of prayer and the power of focusing your intention are all very much at play here.

Chapter Fourteen

Prayer in Ritual

There is a lot of variety in Druid rituals, informed by which Order, if any, a group is connected to, and the inclinations of participants. So, all I can do is generalise, and this is not a detailed reflection of everything Druids do.

Druid rituals tend to start with a "hail and welcome" section. Precise contents, order and wording can vary quite a lot between groups. Some gatherings cast circles, and sanctify them, others don't. Some Druids make a call for peace. However, whatever form it takes, there tends to be an opening section about welcoming, honouring, and settling in.

The "meet and greet" opening sections of a ritual can work in a number of ways. I think it's worth pausing to consider what those are, so as to place any prayer aspect in its context. This introductory part of a ritual can be all about seeking permission from the spirits, and engaging their support. We might ask certain energies or entities to be with us, or if we are more Wiccan in style, we might even summon and demand their presence. I find that approach uncomfortable, but there's a whole spectrum of approaches between honouring and demanding, and what makes sense on the day can vary. We can give this opening time to honouring deities, the land, our ancestors and so forth, with no assumption about their presence or interest. Taking the time to consider those other beings serves to make us more aware, and perhaps more likely to hear if there is a second side to the conversation. This setting up period also functions to shift participants from an everyday mind-set, into a more mystical one.

I've experienced many rituals where the repeated refrain of the opening section is "hail, and welcome". The spirits of place were there long before we turned up. The three worlds, four elements, and the directions exist. They do not need us to invite them in. Perhaps the only group we can truly hail and welcome is our own ancestors. It is not the need of spirit or divinity that is really at play here, but the need of humans. Ritual-goers need to open their minds, consider what they are seeking, and dedicate themselves to the business of ritual, as part of transitioning out of whatever they were doing prior to attending. This "hail and welcome" is better viewed not as inviting the spirits in – if there are any. It is the "hail and welcome" of the guest entering another's space. All too often, I think, we lose sight of that. We are the visitors, unless we are working in our own homes. My feeling is that we should not welcome in the spirits of place, especially, but ask them to kindly put up with us for a while. They are the residents, and we are in their space.

Our attitudes to these parts of the ritual inform what we do. The group that summons spirits for magical workings has little use, I suspect, for reverence or prayer. The group that doesn't expect entities to show up, or take interest, may not have much use for a prayer approach, either. There can, however, be areas of overlap between ritual openings and prayer. If the opening section of a ritual is all about opening ourselves to other entities and awareness, or seeking communion with them, a prayer approach can make a lot of sense. The issues I've already raised, of precise language and tone, apply here, too. It is important to think about what we intend, and what we want to have happen.

My own preference is to greet the spirits of place at the very beginning of a ritual, seeking permission, expressing intention and recognising that which already inhabits the ritual space. Callings to elements and ancestors also recognises that these simply exist, rather than demanding anything, and here I will ask broadly for tolerance and blessings. The end of a ritual usually revisits the same energies from the opening, with a round of "hail and farewell" (let's not get into the semantics here!). At this point, the expression of gratitude for the experience in ritual is important to me. Both opening and closing words create the possibility of connection. We can go further and ask whatever we have called to, if it will stay with us, to inspire us and show us how best to serve.

There are two standard prayers that seem to reliably come up in Druid rituals I have attended. I've no experience of other groups around the world in ritual, and so have resorted to asking online about this one. Many Druids from further afield do not seem familiar with the standard UK pair, although there are other prayers I am less familiar with that are in use in other places. This next section will be of less use to someone unfamiliar with the prayers I am talking about, but do please use it as a prompt to consider how any standard prayers you are familiar with actually function.

I am unsure of the provenance of, "We swear by peace and love to stand, heart to heart and hand in hand. Mark, oh spirits and hear us now, confirming this, our sacred vow." The internet suggests "author unknown", offers it as traditional Celtic or Irish wedding vows, and offers little by way of either consensus, or a suggested original. It has the cadence of revival Druidry, to my ear, suggesting as it does something fraternal, without getting too much into the business of actual gods. It's that tell-tale combination of being both passionate, and vague, coupled with a kind of archaic phrasing that may easily be faux-archaic. "Mark, oh spirits" is the language of an imaginary golden age, I rather suspect. I can't prove it though.

My experience has been that this is one is repeated three times in ritual, while everyone holds hands around the circle. It functions as a cheerful confirmation of community. It also means that we need to feel comfortable with the people who make up our circles. A back-stabbing from someone who has sworn, heart and hand in this way, is a particularly painful thing. While the prayer asks unspecified "spirits" to witness it, largely this is an act of dedication to community. Arguably at this point, we are praying to each other. Having shared this prayer many times, I find it powerful and affirming, which is more important to me than where it actually came from.

The second commonly used prayer is generally attributed to Iolo Morganwg, either as the author, or translator, depending on inclination to trust the dear old fraudster (from which you can tell where I sit on this one!). There are a number of versions in circulation, but the gist of it goes like this... *"Grant, oh spirits, thy protection, and in protection strength, and in strength understanding, and in understanding knowledge, and in knowledge, the knowledge of justice, and in the knowledge of justice the love of it, and in the love of it, the love of the Gods and Goddesses, and in the love of the Gods and Goddesses, the love of all existences and all goodness."* Sometimes a *so may it be* gets slapped on the end, for good measure.

This prayer, interestingly, seems prone to "folk processing". Being longer, people tend to forget bits and swap in odd words they find preferable. Spirits, gods, and goddesses float in and out. There are versions that open "grant, oh God," or "Grant, oh Gods," which have very different tones. I've heard it rewritten as a prayer to the ancestors. During my period with Bards of the Lost Forest, we found issues with the ending in terms of how divinity is represented (if at all) and the ordering of spirit, existence and goodness was not something we were able to agree on. The love of all existences leading to love of all goodness and thence love of the gods makes as much sense as the other way. The result tended to be a beautifully chaotic finale as we all went with whatever version we liked best. Collective prayers do not have to be tidy, shared murmurings of the same stuff. There is no loss in expressing diversity, and I cannot imagine nature is offended by chaos. Heartfelt prayers are more important than uniform ones.

The "grant oh spirits" prayer (also called the Gorsedd prayer) was actually the basis of my first attempt at writing something substantial on the subject of Druidry. The project failed, utterly, and it was a while before I worked up the nerve to write *Druidry and Meditation* instead. In the context of creating this book, I have realised that failure on my part is both interesting and relevant. I spent a lot of time working with "grant, oh spirits", voicing it on a daily basis. This led me to contemplating the many transitions the prayer asks for, wanting to understand how that would work on a person. I thought a great deal about what it means to ask for protection. What are we asking to be protected from, at this point? It isn't specified. What are the implications of seeking protection? It is one thing using the prayer in times of difficulty, when *grant oh spirits thy protection* becomes a ritualised way of begging *make this bad thing stop!* In a calm and peaceful ritual, the words make less sense.

The transition from protection to strength makes a tad more sense. Being protected, we might grow as plants do when sheltered from the frost. Asking for strength makes a lot of sense anyway. Inner strength enables us to cope with what life throws our way and is a good virtue to cultivate.

In strength... understanding. Here I faltered a little. What gives us the transition from strength to understanding? Do we mean that in a sense of growing compassion or comprehension? That makes more sense as a consequence of experiencing vulnerability, more than strength. Understanding can indicate sympathy or an intellectual grasp, but neither feels like a satisfying step onwards from achieving strength. I'm not convinced that the ambiguity is a useful prompt to deeper thinking. Then, if the understanding is intellectual in many ways the following reference to knowledge is a reiteration, not anything new. Compassion can lead to knowledge, but I think it's more likely to flow the other way; we are compassionate when we have knowledge of what it is like to suffer.

Then knowledge begets the knowledge of justice – of all the things we might come to know about. Justice does not occur in nature very reliably, we have to make our own, and often fail. The knowledge of justice is a wonderful aspiration, a good aim for a Druid, if we take it as "the knowledge of what justice means and therefore how to live justly". The knowledge of justice leads us to the love of it. Why? It is surely more important and productive to love the idea of justice in face of not experiencing it. We need to make our own justice, and we can't expect the gods to magically provide it – this is a human responsibility. Justice is all about our relationships with each other, no intervention can give us what we do not make for ourselves. For me, much of the point of nature religion is not to be dealing with gods who keep score and dish out punishment and reward.

Loving all existences seems fine to me as a general premise, but then we run into "all goodness". That's a very subjective idea. Furthermore, loving what is good is not especially difficult, and we really shouldn't need to ask for help with that one. The things that most need our love are not good, but flawed, failing and sometimes entirely wrong. To love that which needs loving is important, rather than just loving that which is straightforward.

The more time I spent analysing the prayer, the more problematic I found those transitions. We use this prayer in ritual because it is one of the few collective prayers people are passably able to agree on (although plenty of people don't use it). However, it is a deeply flawed piece of writing. It doesn't invite mystery and it shows precious little gratitude. It is simply a stream of petition for things that don't really add up. The reason for this, I eventually discovered, is that it was a prayer with a context. It was first used at a gathering where Iolo and his people were under real threat of physical violence.[24] With the image of threatened and surrounded Druids in mind, the whole thing takes a different tone. It makes a lot more sense, too. The call for protection and strength in face of enmity, the call for understanding and insight – perhaps as much in the hearts of those who threatened them as in the Druids themselves. "In the knowledge of justice, the love of it" becomes a potent challenge when the people poised to act unjustly are in earshot. I gather it worked, one way or another.

The prayer itself becomes an illustration of what happens when we take someone's words out of context. It loses sense. Perhaps framing it by reminding people of the context in which it was first spoken, would make a difference. Perhaps if we say that prayer, picturing the people who are not acting safely or justly in our lives, it might gain more weight again.

I had a shot at re-writing it, just to see what I could come up with, using the same shape but trying for follow-ons that I could make sense of.

Grant, oh spirits, thy protection, and in protection, insight, and in insight, understanding, and in understanding, compassion, and in compassion rightful action, and in rightful action the love of it, and in the love of it, the love of all existences, and in the love of all existences, a sense of the sacred, and in that sacredness, peace.

If you like it, feel free to use it. However, what I suggest is sitting down with the original (or whatever version you have) and making your own journey through the possible transitions to see what makes sense to you. Perhaps the most important aspect is working out where you want those transitions to take you. On different days you might be drawn to different words and journeys. It is worth remembering that these prayers are just some words a person put together, and that anyone can assemble an equally valid prayer, or for that matter, a better one.

Dedications

Bardic dedications can feature as part of a ritual. Druid gatherings at both Avebury and Stonehenge certainly used to feature them and I assume they are available at other places, too. I initiated as a Bard of Cor Gawr (Stonehenge) and Caer Abiri (Avebury). The names may be more revival than ancient, but I was new to Druidry and it all seemed pretty impressive and important at the time. The awe inspired by the setting, the drama of it and my inexperience, conspired such that when I repeated back the words of the dedication, on my knees in the dawn dew at Stonehenge, palms to the sacred earth, these were potent prayers. The actual words passed through me, leaving only the knowledge that I had sworn to be a bard of the land and that I felt myself to be properly on the Druid path as a consequence. I wasn't a Druid, but I was learning.

It wasn't until I started leading bardic initiations for Bards of the Lost Forest, and rededicated as a bard in that group, that the words registered with me. I'm recollecting as best I can, because the internet has failed to provide... "We assemble on the Gorsedd mound of mother earth. We gather in the light of the sun, the eye of enlightenment. We assemble at (insert time and place) to constitute ourselves a gathering of the bards of Britain". On it went in this vein. It's not the only bardic initiation out there, OBOD's is wholly different and no doubt other Orders have their own approaches. This one turns up in fragments all over the place and, back around 2005, I was able to track the whole text down online. I've been through a few computers since then, and I don't have it. These days, it isn't as available, which is interesting, but it had a wide influence in the UK and certainly travelled to some groups in America; Caer Pugetia seemed to be using it, for one.

This influential and quite widely used bardic initiation was not the words for an individual, but for a whole group "we gather to constitute ourselves" is the key line here. I did some research, years ago, and came to the conclusion that the script then in use at Avebury and Stonehenge, at British Druid Order rituals, and later Druid Network rituals, was cobbled together for the first significant 20th century gathering at Avebury. That event was created by Philip Shallcrass and Emma Restall Orr. Some of the words had been borrowed from revival Druidry. There were bits of Native American origin, and probably some original bits as well. As the paper trail was all online, I can't offer much by way of hard evidence. It may still be out there, but I do not know where, and the internet is made of shifting sands, and kittens. I didn't do a deep, academic delve at the time, I was searching for spiritual reasons, not writerly ones. It was enough for me, at the time, to grasp that this wasn't something ancient, sacred and untouchable. It was a hodge podge that didn't make much sense when properly considered. This gave me the push I needed to create my own initiation that might help someone new to the path make a formal dedication to study, and ask to be inspired.

What I wrote became an expression of what I think it means to be a bard. It included dedication to service, and a request for blessings. I kept the bits of the old version that appealed to me. The result was a prayer, a drama of transition, an act of public ritual and it seemed to inspire the people who undertook it. I won't share it, because anyone who has walked the bard path for a time could write something similar. If you feel equal to the work of initiating new bards, you really should be bard enough yourself to write some decent words for them.

Prayer in ritual, as with the example of bardic initiation, isn't always a clearly defined thing. Prayer is a form of ritual in its own right. Dedication and celebration can be forms of prayer. I don't think there's much to be gained in getting bogged down in the definitions. If it helps you to understand something in terms of it being prayer, go that way. If you find it unhelpful to view something as a form of prayer, articulate it to yourself in some other way that makes more sense. We can pray to traditions, to forms of energy and to ideas as well as to more obvious manifestations of the divine.

Group prayer is a very different business from praying alone. If you pray privately then you speak for yourself. Praying collectively can tie everybody into one set of words. If people attending a ritual are unhappy with prayers being offered for them by others, this can cause a lot of tension. Imagine what would happen if an evangelical, fundamentalist Christian were able to pray in a Druid circle. They'd probably be asking God to rescue us from the clutches of Satan and show us the light. It is a far-fetched example, deliberately. Open rituals and Druid circles often attract non-Druids and inexperienced learners. What happens if a Wiccan attendee prays to The Goddess as though speaking for the whole circle? Or a Heathen invokes a deity half the circle hasn't heard of? Or someone calls to a Hindu god? There are issues of etiquette and precise language use here.

Druids are a varied lot. A normal Druid circle could realistically expect a mix of hard and soft polytheists, animists and pantheists. The odds are good that there may be some agnostic, non-theist, duotheist and part-Druid-part-something-else participants. Your "Druidry and x" people can bring Christian, Buddhist, Shinto, Shamanic, Heathen and Wiccan influences as the most likely extras, but potentially just about anything. Thus every individual in the circle will probably have a slightly different take on Druidry, some of which cannot be aligned into one shared world view. Further, there are differences between those who focus on Welsh and Irish source material, there's continental Druidry, and evolving non-European traditions. Different Orders have different approaches and a circle can have Druids from different Orders. Even in an entirely hard polytheist circle, the odds are not everyone honours the same gods in the same way.

It is possible, if not likely, that the deities honoured by the participants at any given ritual are not compatible. If we asked them to all show up, and they did, there might be trouble. Even within pantheons, it doesn't always make sense to invoke a lot of different deities. If you take the mythology seriously, then you'll know that getting involved in the many disputes of deities is not a good idea for mere mortals.

Now, for the person who sees all deities as manifestations of the one great uber being, or one Goddess, or feels that everything is underpinned by love anyway, there is no problem here. However, we do not all share that perspective. There are, as I already mentioned, issues of etiquette here, both in terms of how we treat other people, and how we treat the divine. On both counts, respect matters. I'm not usually stroppy and dogmatic in my thinking, but this is one of the areas of exception. I think this is such an important issue that I'm going to put out some ground rules for approaching group prayer and prayer in ritual.

If you want to work in groups, accept that there is going to be diversity. If you want to only be with people who believe exactly the same thing you do, be prepared to end up working alone. Do not expect anyone to be so overwhelmed by the brilliance of your understanding that they convert at once to your way of doing things.

Start from the assumption that everyone has different beliefs. Even if you think those beliefs may be like a facet of yours, don't speak from that attitude. We may disagree about the meaning of life and death and the nature of our existence and of deity. We are entitled, each of us, to our own beliefs and not to having them rudely shoehorned into someone else's approach.

Do not speak on behalf of others. Do not say "we honour Epona" unless you have checked that everyone in your circle feels able to support this statement. It is rude to the deity to speak inaccurately, and it is rude to those around you to make dedications on their behalf without their informed consent. "I honour Epona" is fine.

If you are leading rituals, where possible give everyone the chance to speak their own words, to their own deities, using the names they prefer. Or to speak as animists, or as pantheists, or however makes sense to them. If people in your ritual unwittingly break the first three rules, take them aside privately at some other time and explain the etiquette. Do not challenge them publically, that's also rude, and not respectful to their gods, either. We can treat people and deities with respect regardless of whether we believe in them, or agree with them.

As I understand it, the ancient Celts were more likely to say things such as "I swear by the Gods my people swear by" than to name them. Relationship with deity can be a very personal thing. In public prayer it may make more sense to avoid voicing names, and speak more euphemistically and inclusively.

I swear by all that I hold sacred.

May your deities watch over you.

We can talk broadly about sacredness, divinity and spirit. We can talk individually about gods, goddesses, spirits, ancestors, or any other term that makes sense to us. It may seem pale, but it can be a good deal more personal. You know what you mean and whoever you are honouring should know too. Taking a gentler approach to the language makes ritual more inclusive. We can then focus on sharing the areas of commonality rather than having group prayers flag up problematic differences. I care more about your wanting to be there than I do about how or if you name your gods, or what you'd make of my own curious mix up.

There are exceptions. One would be the ancestors – we all have them, so invoking them in ritual is not too complicated so long as we are alert to the diversity of ancestry people may have. We all share the ancestors of the place we are in at that moment. The other reliable one to put in the mix is the spirits of place. Rituals happen in a place, that place has spirits. If you honour the tangibles – wind, sun, earth, plants, etc. (or that which is just outside, for an indoor ritual) and suggest the unseen, everyone should be able to find their own way of making sense of that.

We may find limits to our tolerance and our capacity for respect. That's a very personal issue, but the one thing I would say is this: do not stand in ritual with people you neither like nor respect. It doesn't work, and it can prove damaging. If someone publically calls on a deity you feel uncomfortable about, you have to find a way of dealing with that. There are no rules for handling this one, save that everything you do is an expression of your Druidry, so walk it and talk it in times of conflict, too.

Many people who come to ritual have prior experience of Christianity. Most of our wider cultural assumptions about prayer come from these Christian influences. This can be problematic. For those who want their Paganism to be all about magical rites and spells, prayer as a term can evoke everything they wanted to get away from. The idea of it can be off-putting. However, what is ritual without an attempt to connect with something beyond ourselves? What is prayer, if not an attempt at connection? If we rediscover prayer as attempting to communicate with the sacred, rather than as something one faith has a monopoly on, or that serves some irrational and superstitious function, its place in Druidry becomes more apparent.

One simple solution is to stay away from the word "prayer" when undertaking group ritual. We can explore the process of communing and listening, without bringing all the baggage along that can go with the word. It might be a better alternative to make time when each person can say what they are grateful for, or can dedicate themselves to forms of service. Many aspects of ritual suggest prayer without naming a recipient. If we make a call for peace, "May there be peace in the east", we don't specify who is being asked to make that happen. Clearly, action is called for, conscious engagement is implied. But whose?

It is not the job of a Druid in ritual to make anyone do it our way. It is not our place to poke others toward deities, or dedicate them to anything without their requesting it. Nor is it our place to convert people to animism, nontheism, polytheism, or anything else. It is not our work to make anyone pray for anything in particular, or to anything in particular. Any such efforts are at odds with serving our communities. It is when people start imagining that their gods require them to do things to other people, and make other people do things to please said gods, that the trouble starts. If it is disrespectful, it's not very Druidic. The time for disrespect is in the face of tyranny, cruelty, oppression, arrogance and irresponsibility. We can and must differentiate between healthy diversity and unreasonableness.

Whether present as a leader or as a participant, the role of the Druid is always to inspire and facilitate. Give other people space in which they can find their own understanding, and encourage them to voice it. If what they come up with doesn't look anything like Druidry to you, that's absolutely fine. Maybe they aren't Druids. Maybe they are some other kind of Druid.

Prayer in ritual can be used to direct people. It can be a tool of control. There is no spiritual value in making people do things that do not agree with them.

Chapter Fifteen

My Work is My Prayer

Thus far, I've been focusing on verbal prayer. Partly because Druidry is quite word orientated, partly because I am too. I find it difficult to do anything without putting it into words at the same time, articulating things inside my head. My thoughts run in a way comparable to narration, usually with a single, coherent thought stream. On rare occasions it is less coherent in here, and there's more jumping about. I mention this because I am not well qualified to discuss non-verbal prayer. I cannot do anything much without layering on those verbal thinking habits.

It is my understanding that not everyone lives in a world of words, and that for many, a less wordy approach will make more sense. In this chapter, I'll be looking at ways in which non-verbal prayer can function, bearing in mind that most of the time I'm writing from a position of taking interest, not from experience.

Non-Verbal Prayer Traditions

There are many examples from around the world of prayer methods that are not made of words. Many faiths have ways of expressing gratitude, worship or reverence that do not call for linguistic expressions. Both Shinto and Hinduism have complex rituals around offerings to deity, and my understanding is that in Hinduism, such acts of devotion are considered more important communications with the divine than verbal prayer. It is very easy to lie with words, and humans will lie in prayer too – especially around intention. The old chestnut of *let me have this one favour, Gods, and I promise to...* Often such promises are neither meant nor honoured. All too frequently when we seek to bargain with deity, we do not hold up our side of the deal. By contrast, when we give our time to acts of devotion, there are no two ways about it; we are doing something.

It is possible to repeat words without considering them. Bodily actions are that bit harder to ignore. The more complex and involved an activity is, the less scope we have for doing it carelessly. This seems to be precisely the logic underpinning Tai Chi, yoga, and sacred dance. We might also attribute the same impact to the involved physical process of Islamic prayer. Using the body engages us in the moment, giving realness and weight to what we do. Thoughts can be flighty, ephemeral things. Prayers made of action are more substantial in ways that we ourselves cannot hope to ignore.

If your whole being is engaged in an activity that requires mental attention, then you have brought your entire self to the process. You have also brought time into the equation. Of all the things available to us, time is the most precious. We only get to use it once. Aside from our bodies, it is the only thing we truly own.

I have a lot of difficulty with offerings as a concept. How does taking one bit of manifest spirit somewhere and putting it in front of another bit of spirit make that an offering from us? Offerings work when you see a distance between this world and deity, but when you understand spirit as manifest and present, it's less meaningful. The apples, feathers, flowers and crystals of a typical offerings altar do not belong to the people who brought them. Each is a thing, and a spirit in its own right. How can we meaningfully give that which is not ours to begin with? Where is the meaning in killing a flower in order to lay it before a standing stone? The sacrifice is not ours, but the flower's. Why should we demand that of another living thing? Our time and our bodies, however, we can give.

When we attempt a dialogue with the sacred, through a physical process that involves our time, prayer becomes an act of direct engagement. While I still bring my wordiness to this, there is clearly no requirement for language. These are not the prayers of trying to say something to deity, but of trying to listen. Often, the more inner silence we can bring, the better. I find this difficult. The inside of my head appears to be made of words. Still, I know how to listen to wordy humans, so there are things I can try to do here.

I find bodily engagement difficult. I have spent a lot of years trying not to notice my body, tuning out pain and pushing through fatigue. I've learned to blot out unwelcome things, done to me against my will. I have learned, as a survival strategy, not to be overly present in my own flesh. This may have contributed to living in my head in a reality made of words. However, a number of experiences over the past year have encouraged me to re-think this arrangement. I've been heavily influenced by Theo Wildcroft's writing and teaching on Sacred Body work – some of which I was able to share on my Druid Life blog. Joanne van der Hoeven's work on Zen Druidry, both through her blog and in her book of that title, has influenced me a great deal, too.[25] I've come to consider that my body should perhaps be part of my spiritual life. These have been hard lessons to study.

My body is me, not the separate identity I have treated it as being. It is through my body that I experience the natural world, for my body is both natural and in nature. From the sun on my back as I write, to the water in my stomach, I am in nature. My gods, such as I relate to them, are also of nature. What kind of dialogue can I have if I wilfully exclude parts of my own nature from the process? I've learned to give time to my body on pain reducing work, before I give time to prayer. That means some days I don't even get to the prayer stage. However, I'm working to become that which is more able to engage with existence and that seems more important than upholding a routine. I am allowing myself more time to just stop and be, here, in this body, this space and this moment. As a consequence, I am becoming more receptive to messages from both within and without my skin.

The unawareness I had held was deliberately constructed to help me deal with trauma. Peeling off the shell I have created, which is a many-layered thing, means feeling vulnerable and exposed. This lump of flesh, so shameful to me, unwanted by me, is also the only thing enabling me to experience the world. I have had to start learning how to inhabit myself in order to do anything else of any significance.

In the process of becoming more aware of my body, I discovered archaeological layers of emotional pain and old grief. This is not what I wanted, nor did I want to face it, own it, or deal with it, but the process that grew out of prayer gained its own momentum. I could not have stopped it, had I tried, I suspect. I know that I need to go through it, but not what lies beyond.

I am aware of a few other people who are deliberately not in their bodies. Souls gazing out through the veil of flesh, never fully here, never at ease with themselves. I know plenty of people who do not do anything much to involve the mind with the body. Many aspects of modern, western culture encourage this. We are not present in our bodies when passively watching television. Sitting in vehicles is nothing like independent movement. Offices keep us still and desk bound. Computers let us pretend to be alive while our own skin is forgotten. How many people are not present to themselves?

To be a Pagan who cannot relate to nature as it manifests in the form of your own body, is to be in trouble. I write that from experience. If we cannot honour our bodies as nature, what hope have we of honouring the rest of the world? My body is not separate from nature, or from spirit. How can I pray if I am not present in my own skin?

Like many people, I have been taught to feel ashamed of my body – its shape, output, hair, smells, wrinkles, wobbly bits, rough bits. We are all being sold irrational ideals with a side order of self-hatred. If I buy into the idea that my flesh isn't good enough, how can I hope to work with it in a sacred way? It becomes increasingly clear to me that spiritual work is going to require re-owning my body.

This skin is as nature, time and life have made it. This skin is good enough. This body bore a healthy child, it fetches shopping, it carries what is needed and does the work. It is not an infinite resource, but it is good enough. This face is no worse than anyone else's. If I could just hold onto those concepts for more than a few seconds at a time, I would be getting somewhere.

Time given to reclaiming the body, is spiritual work. Overtly calling that time a dedication to the sacred and an act of prayer can help us take it more seriously, which in turn is useful. If we are working on, and with, the nature of our own bodies, the gods of nature may hear us. And really, these are nature gods; mud, shit, sweat, spit, semen and blood really shouldn't offend them. I may be fat and hairy, but so are badgers and bears. Most of nature is not perfect, by the cosmetic standards of modern humans.

Everything Can Be a Prayer

There's a rather amusing tendency in archaeology to assume anything lacking an obvious use, is religious. Conversely, anything with inbuilt utility is not likely to be also assigned a religious function. We have a language that readily separates the sacred from the profane, and the mundane from the magical. We also draw lines between religious and secular activity. In this binary way of thinking, this world of either/or, religion is what you do when you aren't doing anything useful.

Part of the problem with religion is this approach that hives it off from "normal life". It gives us religions that exist for an hour or so once a week, when you will also be wearing a nice hat. Our culture has been keeping the spiritual out of normal, everyday life for a long time. This isn't about the theoretical separation of Church and State, but about how we practise our beliefs.

Most of the religions I have read about include the scope for making a full-time religious dedication. Often this manifests in the taking up of a monastic lifestyle. To be full-on religious means, for many people, crossing some very clear lines and leaving the everyday concerns behind. It is the beggar monk with robes, bowl and no other earthly possessions. Underfed, eyes gazing into a beautiful distance the rest of us cannot hope to see. It is the life that is full of prayer and singing, but in which you will never have to fill in a tax return. Special clothing, different living arrangements, different rules; the full-time religious life is clearly different from a normal life. Such approaches help reinforce our belief in the divide between that which is sacred, and that which is not.

A great deal of how we experience the world depends on our intentions and feelings. You can chop potatoes in a state of happy contentment, or inner resentment. Either way you get potato slices, but the experience for the one who chops will be radically different in each instance. The happy chopper may have affirmed their love of home, family and spud. The resentful one may have confirmed their status as a put-upon victim. No one else has to notice for this to have real effects on the diminisher of root matter.

Back in my first Druid book, *Druidry and Meditation*, I explored the idea that anything can be the subject of, or a method for, meditating. We can make the deliberate choice to live some, or all, of our lives in contemplative ways. Prayerfulness is also as much a state of mind as anything else. It is a way of relating to what we do and we can adopt it at any time and in any situation.

One option is to offer everything we do to deity. We may do that just the once, at the start of the day, at the start of each activity, or according to some other scheme. I have encountered this approach in both Christian and Buddhist writing. I have not explored it personally because I don't find the idea especially resonant.

We might equally seek to bring an awareness of deity into our lives in whatever we are doing, asking in a process of ongoing petition to do our work well, in ways that please deity or that uphold relevant virtues. Thus it is not the outcome of the work exactly that we offer up, but the spiritually aware approach to it, along with any differences that nuance brings. Working in this way is also a constant petition to live more in-line with our spiritual intentions, making our actions better reflect our beliefs or values. Arguably when we do this, we are praying more to our own better, or higher, selves than to any external manifestation of the divine.

Everything we do brings us into contact with other living beings. With an animist perspective, everything we do automatically engages us with other manifestations of spirit. Everything is about such relationship and it all brings scope for meaningful exchange. If everything we do becomes prayer, then we should be listening to what is around us, with the intention to walk more lightly, cause less harm, use less, and live more harmoniously.

It is easy to feel spiritual about uplifting things encountered in lovely places. I think there can be considerably more impact, however, from taking spiritual intent into ostensibly mundane situations. For a start, doing so helps to erode the religion/not-religion illusion. It is ludicrous to think that, if there are gods, they only care about what we do at specific times and in certain places. The religion of once a month with freshly polished shoes, fails to recognise that life is a full-time job. Part-time religion will not keep up with actual life. Bringing spiritual intention to allegedly normal life, changes us. It allows us to re-imagine the world as a sacred and meaningful place. Nothing needful can seem beneath us if we can also see how it is sacred. Nothing living can be irrelevant or worthless when we anticipate a presence of spirit or deity. The definitions of "mundane" and "banal" can be re-drawn. That which was ordinary becomes imbued with value.

The act of bringing, or trying to bring, prayer to everything, has profound consequences. Holding a sense of sacredness suggests awe, and inspires love. The worm in the road, the feckless human next door, the person who just insulted you online, the rat in the attic. Where do you stop? When do you get to say, everything is sacred apart from this one bit over here...? You don't. That can be challenging and uncomfortable. It makes deliberate cruelty and destructive carelessness very difficult to justify. The splendid paradox of becoming both more tolerant and more intolerant at the same time certainly keeps life interesting.

In practice, of course, it is not a case of getting up one morning and deciding to treat everything as sacred and thereafter making everything you do into a prayer. Try that and the most likely outcomes are either that you'll overthink yourself into inaction, or forget and stop doing it by lunchtime. Habits of thought and action do not change overnight on a whim. If you want to reach a place where all action is also prayer, it has clearly got to be a process. Pick small and viable things to focus on and extend gradually. Expect to take years. It requires total mindfulness of self in all things, plus total attention to everything else. I am a long way short of having the personal awareness, the empathy or the focus to make everything I do an act of prayer. Perhaps if I get there – twenty or thirty years hence doesn't seem preposterous if I really work at it – I'll come back and explain how to do it with the benefit of some actual insight.

New Age thinking is often keen to tell us that we can become totally enlightened beings, quickly. We can't. We grow slowly, like trees. It takes years of sustained effort often, to make any noticeable change at all. Often the first lesson of a spiritual path is to slow down, and be patient with yourself. It is okay that your brow is not shining with wisdom yet. It is fine that gods do not show up in person to answer your prayers. This is a journey, and it is a long walk made of many steps. The further we go, the better able we become to see how small a distance we have walked compared to the vast swathe of walkable landscape available to us. Everything can be a prayer, but not today.

But Is It Really Prayer?

The line *my work is my prayer* is easily announced. Looking at someone from the outside, it isn't easy to tell if this is really the case. A lot of the time, other people's spiritual lives are no one else's business anyway. Exceptions to this come when someone claims authority, a right to power, or uses their spirituality to justify harassment. When a person is charging for teaching, or otherwise making their spiritual life a public matter, then the integrity of their work is no longer a private issue. Self-honesty also matters. Saying *my work is my prayer* as a justification, to cover for shortcomings or as some kind of cop-out, is not good for the soul.

It is easy to take some mental short-cuts around the issue of prayer. Having established that absolutely everything we do can be prayer, we can take a second step and say *therefore I am doing it already and need make no further effort.* Why put in the time to develop a prayer practice if you can simply identify what you do as prayer already? Why not decide that you don't need to go to all the trouble of learning, or doing anything extra? Your work is good, you've been doing it for a while and it speaks for itself. The more experienced we become, the easier it gets to say *I'm there already* and not explore further. This is not a good thing.

Tai Chi teaches a succession of movements, often called a form. When a person has mastered the form, they do not graduate to learning a grander, more dramatic, more powerful or more difficult form. Instead, they go back to the beginning and learn the same thing again. And again. Going back to the basics, to the core practice, stops us kidding ourselves that we have somehow arrived, or achieved a fantasy status. Every time we go back to the simplest things, we go deeper into what we work on. You can take a similar approach when learning a tune, or undertaking a ritual. It is a mistake, often, to imagine that we graduate from the simplest things and go on to something more important. Often, what we need most is to simplify, coming back to earth and sun, slowing down into this breath, and this moment. Progress means greater insights and a greater sense of meaning and wonder. It does not mean no longer needing to bother with the simple things.

There are no shortcuts or fast tracks in spiritual work. The only pace we can go at is our own, and only we can determine, as individuals, what constitutes progress. It is far too easy to decide that we already know what a thing is, and that we can therefore skip it. The idea that my work is my prayer can be a temptation to skip. Except that, if we approach it in that way, our work probably won't be an act of prayer in the first place.

The idea of our actions functioning as prayers only works if you undertake things with a genuine commitment, and as a spiritual activity. It is very hard to know how to actually do that without going through other forms of prayer a bit first. Based on personal experience, I feel confident saying that prayer as an intellectual premise is wholly different from prayer as a lived experience. I came to this subject out of curiosity, and found very quickly that without doing it, I couldn't hope to understand it. There are a lot of other things in life I found could not be adequately explained second-hand. Only first-hand experience will do when it comes to falling in love, giving birth, going up in a hot air balloon, burning yourself, or having sex, to give a few examples. Granted, having some information about how others found it will give you a passable impression, but the first time you actually burn yourself, or do any of those other things, is nonetheless surprising. War and ecstasy, grief and drunkenness. We do not fully know much in this life until we live it.

Sometimes, the intellectual input is enough to let you know that an experience isn't for you; which is fair enough. Most of us do not need much persuading that we have no desire to suffer. There are plenty of paths we won't choose to walk, and we cannot hope to walk them all. The idea that we can always fill an experiential gap with abstract knowledge and skip on ahead to the next bit, is not a good one though. Reading about sex is unlikely to get you pregnant. Reading about flotation will not enable you to swim. It is all too easy to do what I did, standing outside of prayer, viewing it as an "in the head" thing that could be grasped rationally. A mix of psychology, history, systems of control and cultural habits, surely? A recipe for cake does not make for good eating. There was a life lesson here, not to assume myself capable of understanding something I hadn't done. Too much the word-in-head person, I can be guilty of forgetting that life is more than books.

Going Full Time

I've touched a few times now on the idea of full-time religion, and beyond that to making everything we do an act of prayer. Acknowledging that I've not achieved anything like that level of dedication, I'd nonetheless like to ponder what "full time" might mean.

There are reasons not to go full time. Do we actually want religion intruding on every aspect of our lives? Where there are tensions between religious requirements and personal inclination, there can be an incentive not to be religious at all times. It may be because personal desire takes us towards immoral acts our professed faiths would not condone. Equally, it might be a less compassionate aspect of a faith that we do not want to manifest in our lives. Homosexuality, divorce or polygamy would provide reasons not to be fully religious for either of those reasons, if you were following the teachings of the monotheistic faiths.

For a Pagan, this is unlikely to apply to the same extent. Free from dogma, for the greater part, we construct our own systems of belief and practice. It gives us a lot less scope for hypocrisy. Nonetheless, there are still those who profess Paganism in public and practise domestic abuse at home. Or those whose honourable relationships only hold firm when there's nothing that seems more important going on. We all encounter the occasional Pagan who is not practising what they claim to believe.

We all do it to some extent though. All forms of Paganism are underpinned by the understanding that nature is sacred. However, we develop our path or practice, the idea of nature being sacred should, logically, inform everything else. This is where we all, to some degree, undertake to be part-time believers. We work for unethical companies because we need the money, and buy unethical foods because we can't afford the alternatives. We send waste to landfill, buy what we do not need, use cars, and put carbon into the atmosphere for trivial, self-indulgent reasons. We buy products developed through animal testing and products that contribute to polluting and destroying the planet. We put excrement into water systems, polluting what should have been drinkable. The quest for ease and comfort has us buying cheap products from unethical sources. We add to human, animal and environmental misery all the time. I am guilty of these things.

To be a full-time Druid in a constant state of prayer and communion with the natural world, simply would not allow us to do that. Most of our justifications for our non-Druidry come from the idea of need. *I need to be economically successful. I need my car. I need all this stuff I am buying.* To take an honest look at both nature and impact is to question all cultural norms. Most of us westerners have far more material wealth than we need, even those of us in relative poverty. There's a culturally ingrained loss of perspective that really takes some challenging.

The other significant underpinning, is envy. Other people have cars, so why not me? Other people take airplane flights to holiday destinations all the time. Other people have flat screen TVs and Xboxes and have covered their gardens in decking and plastic furniture. (That's going to date me, in years to come!) Why have I got to do without? Why must I be the one to make a sacrifice? It's not like my not-buying a microwave will save the world. Why should I miss out on all the good stuff?

This is why most of us are part time. To be a full-time Druid is to see and respect the sacredness of all things. At which point, our whole notion of what is fair and reasonable behaviour has to change. The idea of owning land, or owning an animal, starts to seem preposterous. Ownership is one of the fantasies of consumerism and it allows people to put fences around "property" and believe those fences mean something. Seeing the world in this way is dangerous. It is heresy against capitalism. In taking on such an understanding, you step away from the consuming consensus in a way that will invite them to mock you, at best. That's a very big leap, and holding that perspective about everything, all the time, is alienating, and requires you to behave in ways that other people will not find acceptable.

How can you be in spiritual communion with something you are abusing? Our pollution and self-indulgence can be a barrier to relationship. Or, if we overcome our actions to be more aware of the world, those actions become uncomfortable and intolerable. I have a friend who cannot bear to get into a car. It doesn't make for an easy life.

Imagine needing to know where everything you buy comes from and how it was made, and how it will be dealt with when its working life is done. Imagine having to contemplate everything that comes into your life to be sure it is needed and properly deployed. Contemplating every word spoken for appropriateness, compassion and whether it is good enough to lay before the divine. Learning to think your Druidry, to breathe it and walk it, to dance it through every moment of wakefulness and right through your sleep as well. That's full time and I am not even close to achieving it. We cannot separate our use of nature from our spiritual work with nature and still claim to be wholly dedicated. The plastic packaging in our dustbins says we are misguided.

Most of us will never be full time in our spirituality. Most of us won't achieve enlightenment either, or unravel the secrets of the universe. Expecting perfection is a way of denying humanity. We are flawed. We are always going to struggle with questions of need and sufficiency. All we can hope to do, in any aspect of our lives, is to strive and develop.

Every change we make, matters. Every time we manage to hold greater awareness than before, something changes. Each occasion of trying to be less exploitative of and more in tune with the rest of nature, contributes something. Just a bit of prayer, a bit of recognising sacredness, moves us, creates change and enables more. All of it is worth doing.

I face these issues constantly in my work. I own a small computer with a plastic case and mined minerals inside it. I use electricity in my quest to earn a living. My books are printed, and the graphic novel was printed in China, with all the human welfare issues that raises. Inks are not very eco-friendly. All that stuff is being put into the world on my account. The chemicals used, the trees, the fuel to transport them, and for what? Surely there are better ways to earn a living? Is my day job in any way compatible with my beliefs? It's a question I keep coming back to. I believe in the power of books to re-enchant, inspire, educate and uplift. Stories get in under the radar to influence people. Part of my Druidry drives me to want to contribute beauty, insight and worth to the world. But at what cost? It makes me intensely self-conscious, especially with the fiction. If trees are going to die for the sake of a story, the story ought to be worthy of that. I cannot say with confidence that my work justifies killing trees. On the other hand, I will not put brain-dead, content free, predictable and worthless words out there for any money. I will not make anything I consider to be just marketable pap. It has to be more than a grab for cash, or it is unbearable to me. This has put me at odds with my former agent, and some other publishers. It may well have reduced my scope to make money. *Twilight, Fifty Shades of Gray*, and books that tell you life can be made perfect with ten minutes a day of minimal effort, sell. That I would rather be poor and obscure than successful on those terms is my Druidry showing up, but if I was really full-on, I'd have stuck to the oral tradition and never written a book in the first place.

The more aware we become, the more visible such conflicts of interests in our lives become to us. Nothing in this life is simple. Every action and every existence uses something. Where the willow grows, an oak cannot. Deer thrive at the expense of woodland. Predators hunt and eat. Human needs conflict with the needs of other creatures. Nature is full of tensions, pulling in incompatible directions and often balance is nothing more than tensions that hold each other still. Balance is compromise. Outside, everything eats something else, and all returns to the soil to feed the plants. We humans like to think of ourselves as special. We don't want to be eaten, or starved. We want to own and construct our habitats. Human nature and non-human nature conflict – this too is natural. Our inability to accept anything short of total species victory in all scenarios, is a lot of the problem.

I speculate that becoming a full-time Druid would ultimately lead to seeing yourself as just another bit of the world – not special or entitled. That might make us more willing to accept death when it comes, and more able to give up on this futile collective attempt to somehow stand outside of nature. What that would mean in practice, I cannot begin to imagine.

Chapter Sixteen

What Changed?

Prayer has to do something if it is any way a valid way to spend your time. Whether the process of prayer is magical or psychological is less relevant than whether it gets you somewhere. I have been my own case study for the duration of the book process, from early research to final drafts. Psychology and other sciences do not rate a case study of one, and rightly so. I am not a statistically significant sample, and I was not experimenting in controlled circumstances. Other aspects of my life were in radical flux as I worked on this book. I was attempting to recover from historical trauma, whilst dealing with very high levels of ongoing stress and some hefty life challenges.

It is not easy to draw simple lines between cause and effect when it comes to real life. A lot has changed for me. Was that because my prayers were being answered? Was it because the dedication I made to prayer work fundamentally shifted my outlook? Did the process of prayer indeed serve to strengthen me and develop inner resources? Could there be an element of placebo effect? I took up regular prayer and my life became progressively easier. A number of things that I really wanted have fallen into place. People I had daydreamed about getting to work with, and admired from afar, are now a regular part of my life. A perfect job landed in my lap. An ideal place to live turned up in just the right time frame, as did the means to part company with my boat. So many really important things have fallen into place in the past year and a half. There have been stresses and challenges, but I've become increasingly able to handle them. I can't tell you that prayer achieved this, and if it did, I could not tell you how or why that happened. There were changes, and they continue, and I expect more. I have no idea what comes next.

Theory Becoming Practice

Throughout the book, I've commented on this shift from thinking to doing, whenever I've spotted it, but it is important enough to merit a proper exploration. Over a year before coming to write these words, I started thinking about how prayer does not seem to be that central a feature in Druidry. My initial impression was that it was of greater significance to other religions. Wondering if we might be missing something, or whether there were very good reasons not to pray, I started reading around. Up until this point I had simply equated prayer with petition – in my case offered in times of difficulty and to little effect. So I came to this project "knowing" that prayer does not work. I came as a sceptic, looking for the social and psychological dimensions. I discovered that there are far more books of prayers than ever there are books about what it means to pray. At this point, I clicked into author-mode: I would write a book about the process and concept of prayer. I envisaged something calmly intellectual. Initial, informal talking online suggested Druids were not that interested in prayer. Those that were, tended to come from the hard, polytheist background, where the logic of prayer is underpinned by belief in the literal existence of the gods. This left me expecting to write a book along the lines of, Druids don't pray much because there's really no point in it and we're wise to that.

When I found John Pritchard's work, (written from an Anglican perspective) I started to realise that prayer can be more than petition. This fuelled my academic interest. I read further books and articles, talked to more people online and assembled a big pile of notes.

By slow degrees I began to realise that I did not understand what I was reading. Prayer made no sense to me. It seemed pointless and stupid. On some level it actually made me feel angry. The more smug and self-important the prayer material I found to read, the more angry I became. The more certain and definite an author was, the more I wanted to dismantle the whole thing, atheist style. However, the atheists have already stomped their way through the subject of prayer, and I can get just as irritated by smug atheist disbelief as by any other kind of self-satisfied certainty. It was a case of quit, or step up to really tackling the subject. If I wanted to understand, I was going to have to experiment, and pray, every day.

It wasn't easy. Aside from vague ideas of "nature gods", I had no one to pray to, and I did not really believe in the whole anthropomorphic personification thing anyway. I went into the experiment slow and wary, and stumbled about a lot in fairly random directions. However, I'm a bloody-minded sort of person who does not give up easily. This helped a lot.

Early on I was significantly challenged by my own doubts and disbelief. I had been trending for a long time towards not quite nontheism, more a sense that any deities out there really didn't care anyway. This was in part a direct consequence of the way I was struggling in the rest of my life. It is much easier to believe that you are beloved of the deities during times of ease and success.

Looking around me, I started to notice that the people who are most generous, most honourable and otherwise most virtuous, are not reliably the ones with the easiest lives. Often it is people who have struggled who exhibit most compassion for others, and those for whom life is easiest that giving is difficult. The idea that there could be a divine reward structure for good behaviour has been ingrained in our culture through Protestant capitalist propaganda, amongst other things. If material wealth is a reward for goodness, the rich must therefore be unquestionably good. Worldly failure as manifest in poverty, illness and suffering are divine punishments for sin and therefore require no intervention. There is a political agenda at work here, not a spiritual one.

My feeling that the world is a harsh and hostile place and that the only possible deities would have to be neutral or disinterested, owed a lot to my life experience. That I was trying to overcome the legacy of abuse is not irrelevant here. It is worth noting that abusers frequently encourage victims to feel responsible for what has been done to them. People who believe they deserve punishment are a good deal more cooperative as victims. In much the same way, the habit of the excessively rich of blaming the poor for the existence of poverty, serves to make it easy to maintain things as they are. When you stop buying the lies about how it is your fault that you are suffering, it becomes easier to seek and achieve change. This is undoubtedly one of the processes that changed me as I worked on the book.

Theological debates have raged for centuries around issues of the presence and absence of gods. We have probably been wondering about that one from the moment we first imagined that there could be deities. If deity is all knowing and all powerful, why does it let us do the awful things we do? Why did it make us so flawed and bound to mess up in the first place? The Book Religions seem to postulate a God who has given us a sensual world, but who punishes us for enjoying it. There are many ways of trying to make sense of this, none of them I find satisfying. Pagans tend not to believe in a conscious and active uber-deity. Limited, finite gods and goddesses, or spirits, make more sense in relation to life as I experience it. A weave of sometimes conflicting intentions and energies in a self-creating universe allows that there might be deities to experience and work with, but that they do not have absolute power over everything, including over us. In such a vision, there is no grand plan or ultimate explanation, and a lot of room for life to be messy and uncomfortable, and for the right answer to be accepting that and getting stuck in anyway.

I made several profound life-shifts in tandem as I worked on this book. They were related. As I fought my way out of personal crisis a bit, I began to feel more hopeful about life generally. The world seemed less innately hostile. Rejecting the long held belief that I somehow deserved any ill that befell me, I changed my ideas about myself, and my place in the world. By extension, the idea of deity no longer had to be limited to apathetic or hostile beings in order for my life to make sense to me.

I read several books on Shinto, and Wendy Stokes' *The Lightworkers' Circle Guide*. I liked the idea of Kami, from Shinto; wanting to believe there could be benevolent beings of peace and harmony who will help us if we seek them out. Of course they would have to be sought; a benevolent being will not come along and force upon you what it thinks you need. The process has to be collaborative and consensual to be truly benevolent. Taking this on-board, I started asking, inspired also by Wendy Stokes' words about calling to the kind of presence you need rather than getting tied up worrying about personal names.

I made a shift from theory to practice, from deep pessimism to tentative optimism, from a life and psyche in tatters, towards healing. There are no simple lines of cause and effect here, but the changes were many and prayer was certainly a part of the process of change.

Language Shifts

In the first few chapters of the book, you may have noticed that my language use was very cautious. I wrote from a place of deep uncertainty, caveating everything, flagging up all the opportunities to say "maybe". I've been careful in redrafts to try to keep that as it was when I first wrote it, because it is part of my journey. The shift came around Chapter Six: Standing Before the Unknown and had a lot to do with other things occurring in my life. In January of 2013, I stalled on this project, along with just about everything else I was supposed to be doing. The preceding December had been harrowing and exhausting, the winter weather harsh. I had been both bodily and emotionally very ill. By January I had burned out and could see no point in anything I was doing.

At this point, to my absolute surprise, the universe came through for me. Or at least, small bits of it did. It manifested in a rush of love and support from readers on my blog (druidlife.wordpress.com) and in the form of my publisher at Moon Books – Trevor Greenfield. Trevor asked me to write him a Pagan Portal book, a move that gave me back my sense of purpose. Using a lot of the material I had accumulated whilst researching for this book, I wrote *Spirituality without Structure*. The attendant process of analysing the functional differences between following a religion and creating your own path, caused a lot of ideas to coalesce.

Most importantly, at the point when I felt I just couldn't keep going any longer, things happened that shook my grim perceptions. I realised I was surrounded by support and encouragement. Wendy Stokes deserves another mention here; her generosity and kindness were a real inspiration to me. There were many others whose small gestures and comments added up to create a very large influence. I was not going to be allowed to fall and fail. There are plenty of myths about going into the underworld and, eventually, there is a process of coming back. All of a sudden there were glimmers of light and my long walk through hell seemed to be close to ending.

It was not deities, or magic, or prayer that turned my life around. It was people. However, people are spirit too, people are part of the weave that makes up the fabric of the world. Lines of cause and effect are not always simple. This is the problem with gods – they do not show up with fanfares, or burning plant matter, as giant neon signs glow over their head to announce a divine intervention. When we do get the things we were praying for, they turn up in unremarkable brown envelopes through the post, or the answer is casually mentioned by a friend, a coincidence comes or a happy accident. Who can say? When prayers are not answered we can take it as evidence that the gods do not exist, and when they are, that can be carefully explained. It mostly comes down to what you believe in the first place.

I always was a Pagan. "Thou, Nature art my goddess,"[26] has been with me as a thought form for a long time. This is not an issue of belief. We have just the one planet. The sun comes up, the tides turn, eggs hatch, and death catches us all in the end. I didn't make a conscious decision to change my language deployment during this book, but it seems to have happened, nonetheless. Somewhere during the draft phase of early 2013, I shifted from a very cautious kind of language around deity, to much more comfortably throwing in terms like "nature gods". Becoming comfortable with the language was an important part of the process, given my wordy nature. At this point, I had endured some years of being challenged over my mental functioning. I had repeatedly been accused of being irrational, delusional, a fantasist, and this in a context with the potential to have serious repercussions. No, I had no desire to add to that by going about claiming that Pagan nature gods exist and can be interacted with. I was afraid of people labelling me as crazy as it was, in a system where the people who had made me ill with depression and anxiety were then attempting to capitalise on my illness for their own gain.

By January of 2013, this was all behind me and there would be no more invasive scrutiny. I had been criticised to the point of becoming almost unable to function, but I had survived. I started to pull together what self I had left. There was no one remaining in any area of my life who had the means to push me around. There was just one unpleasant organisation I still had to deal with, but I've commented on my battles with Canal & River Trust already. I had at last the mental space necessary in which it was safe to say whatever I felt needed saying. I could believe whatever I wanted to. I also no longer had to contend with bat-shit-crazy claims from people trying to convince me they could kill or cure with the power of their minds. With that in place, I have become more comfortable with the idea of deity, and with the Pagan gods of my ancestors.

The final piece in this part of the puzzle was Judith O'Grady's brave and captivating book *God Speaking*. Judith tackles head on the tension between ideas about mental health and spirituality. We are not supposed to literally hear voices when we pray. Some people do. It is a wonderful book and it gave me courage.

Anxiety and Depression

Back in 2012, my day usually began with a panic attack. I would surface from sleep with my heart pounding and in a state of total terror. Then, before I tried to do anything else, I would have to try to calm myself down in order to figure out how to get up and face whatever difficulties the day had in store for me. I lived with fear and it made me bodily ill. The panic attacks had started years before, and the constant physical experience of fear took the most horrendous toll on my body. I was suffering from depression most of the time as well; largely as a consequence of the anxiety. It isn't easy to explain to the uninitiated what prolonged fear does to the body and mind. I find it to be more of a problem than ongoing pain, and, given that pain has also been a constant feature for years, consider myself qualified to make the comparison. Checking my email made me so afraid I felt sick. So did picking up the post, and having the phone go off. I'd experience the kind of breath-snatching, chest-crushing, heart-pounding panic attacks that quite literally put me on the floor, as part of daily life.

I was sick in body and mind. I had some counselling, which helped a bit. I did some Cognitive Behavioural Therapy, which gave me skills to manage the symptoms. I could have opted for anti-depressants, but didn't. I could have asked to be signed off work and properly diagnosed, but I wanted to work, and so there was never a detailed diagnosis. Short-term drug interventions helped me through some awful times. Part of my difficulty was that the interventions I had access to were designed for people who were either over-reacting to minor triggers, or whose trauma was historical, not on-going. As my issues were both serious and on-going, there was little anyone could do to help me. I was told I would have little scope for healing until I stopped taking additional damage.

During 2012, there was no reprieve for me and the weather was awful. I was getting soaked to the skin on a daily basis, during some periods. I could not take the strain, mentally or physically and the idea of suicide kept turning up in my head, an alluring incubus in my thoughts. Often that seemed like the only possible way of ending my distress. That I neither died, nor had to be sectioned for my own safety, is in no small part due to my husband, Tom, who simply refused to give up on me, and did everything he could to support and protect me. I would not have made it through that period on my own.

I wasn't praying very coherently when I started. My intention was to avoid futile petition, but in reality *let me survive this* and its painful opposite *just let me die* were coming in about equal measure. I wanted justice, and I found none. Where I needed vindication, I found only blame. Where I should have been supported, I was all too frequently betrayed. No, petition prayers do not work. Holding my sense of self together was almost impossible in face of all of this. I fought not to believe all the damning feedback I had from certain quarters. I cannot say it would have been worse if I'd not been praying. As noted before, this is no kind of objective study.

However, there were correlations between activity and outcome that struck me as significant at the time, and still seem valid with hindsight. The point at which I took up daily prayer, was the point at which the panic attacks started to decrease in both force and frequency. There were no other significant changes in the same time frame. After a little while, I stopped waking into panic each day, and the frequency decreased such that by 2013 I was no longer waking into panic at all.

Untriggered anxiety reduced such that it now requires something to actively frighten me before I'll have a panic attack. The effect on my quality of life has been colossal. Waking straight into terror every day is dreadful.

There may be a simple, psychological explanation here. Prayer calms the mind in much the same way as meditation does. That alone might be enough to explain my improved mental health. I deliberately chose to focus on peaceful and harmonious deities whenever I was together enough not to be just whimpering. That too may have simply helped to change my thinking. Looking back, I feel very strongly that by whatever means, prayer strengthened my resilience to emotional and psychological setback, and helped me to heal. What I cannot do is confidently explain the mechanism. I wasn't particularly seeking healing, just survival. It did not seem to make much odds what I thought I was doing; the calming and healing effect of prayer as an activity remained a constant. This inclines me to think that much of the effect can be ascribed to the psychological aspect of praying. I think that, like meditation, prayer itself changes how our minds work. Who we pray to and what we pray for may be of less consequence than the impact of just plain doing it. I remain as certain as I ever get, that you do not need gods, or belief in gods, for prayer to be a useful undertaking.

Prayer has not saved me from depression and anxiety. I still suffer from both to a degree that can be life-impairing some of the time. However, I am a lot better than I was. The suicidal impulse in me is more muted now than it has been at any time before in the last decade. I have become more honest with myself about my feelings and consequently better able to protect myself from people and situations I find toxic. I have learned to recognise my own limitations, and to be more tolerant about the things in myself I perceive as shortcomings. I give less space and time to the people who demand too much of me.

Prayer has taught me greater patience and helped me develop

some much-needed boundaries. It has been part of the multi-faceted process that has enabled me to consider I might be worth protecting in the first place. I have had to fight not to be damned in my own eyes by the judgments of others, but I have started to consider that perhaps I am not totally worthless, and do not deserve to be kicked about in the way that I have been.

What I have now is not a state of imagining I am loved by some all-powerful super-parent. It is enough for me to think that I can be tolerated. I am no less worthy than a blade of grass or a small pebble. I am no less alive than a slug. Not so many years ago, I felt no entitlement to exist at all. Now I can sit with the grass and dirt and small things and feel as much like I belong as they do. This, for me, is a revelation and looking back, it did not take a miracle to get me here. Just that I said, "Hello?" No part of reality registered me as an affront at this point. I was not smited out of existence.

Dear gods of nature, apparently you are willing to put up with me being here. Thank you. Knowing that helps a lot.

Uncertainty

I am willing to say that prayer has had real and discernible effects on me. What I am not going to do is claim that this observation proves anything else. It proves nothing. There are things a person might choose to infer about deity, reality, and the human mind from all of this, but inference is not proof.

I've had some profound experiences whilst working on this book. There have been moments of numinous awareness and feelings of spiritual significance. I can't tell you whether that was wholly manufactured inside my brain, or somehow came in from outside. The effects of lifting my mood and giving me hope were entirely real and had considerable impact on my life.

I could have taken my experiences from the past year or so and decided that they meant something more. I could have interpreted my insights as proof that gods exist, or as proof that I have a higher self, guiding me, or as proof that I have finally gone stark, raving mad. People do all of those things. Personal experience is the only kind most of us are readily convinced by, but that doesn't mean we can be sure of what exactly we experienced, or what it truly signifies. Thoughts, feelings, ideas, inspiration, memory and fantasy all have a reality inside the mind. This informs what we do, and shapes how we experience life. If I call a subset of those mental experiences "deity" it does not establish that any such thing exists outside of my head. After all, I am also a writer of fiction. Right now there are also talking cats, a time machine, bits of a Stone Age village and a monkey butler roaming round in here as well. I can make them so real that it is possible to write about them as though from first-hand experience. Then, when I put those things outside my head, in stories, they become real to other people. Actually, the monkey butler came out of someone else's head first (Paul Alborough/Professor Elemental, who has been one of the many previously unimaginable blessings to enter my life in the past few years). There are aspects of being a creative human that cannot be usefully discussed in terms of realness. That may be where the gods live.

I can talk about deity, Kami and nature gods. I know that nature exists, and I know that ideas have impact and that a wizard boy who grew up inside someone's mind has the power to change other children's lives. That you probably know I'm referring to Harry Potter further makes my point. Dreams of what could be. Inspiration for that which we may do ourselves. Hope, strength, courage. The real and unreal, possible and impossible. There are things that it is a nonsense to talk about in terms of their "realness".

I am enough of a Celt to love the liminal places. I come towards the end of this book process still clutching my uncertainties. I like my in-between places, my maybes and perhaps. I like my doubts and all the things I can never feel are proved. I like the way that gives me no material to beat other people round the head with and no authority, no "god given" right to tell anyone else what they should be doing.

I like prayer. I'm not angry with it any more. I'll keep doing it, keep asking and searching, doubting and wondering.

Coda

There is a final story to tell, and it is a tricky one because it does not sit tidily with the other things in this book. All the way through, I've been talking about my spiritual life, my uncertainty and maybeism. To do this, I have cheated just a little bit. Partly for my comfort, partly because there is an old story that I simply did not know how to think or feel about, much less tell. I realise that only in coming to this last tale, am I able to finish this book. It's been a process that uncannily seems to have its own agenda.

I was not always agnostic. I cheated in some of what I wrote: I discounted everything that happened in my teens. All those strange, inexplicable times in the hard polytheist days of my youth, when the sacred was real to me, present and accessible. I grew up; not in a good way, but in self-defence, denying the magical simply because I could not bear the way in which it was being used around me, and against me. What can a person do in face of another human being who literally believes themselves to be a god, and who wants to weave your deeply held belief and experience into the ugly fabric of their dysfunction? What do you do with someone who tells you they are the reason one of your friends now has an incurable disease, and that without their on-going magical intervention, one of your other friends would die? I had to deal with more than one genuinely crazy person using the idea of magic as a tool to frighten and control me. It wasn't pretty. In protecting myself, I lost a lot of things along the way. I lost a great deal of innocence, my sense of sacredness, my ability to talk to the divine. Fragments of self and soul were hacked off, or hastily abandoned in a desperate attempt to stay functional.

Those were not good times.

I could no longer trust the memory of my early days, when the world around me hummed and glowed with numinous potential. That too seemed dangerous, and too close to the sickness I needed to protect myself from. I came to ignore my intuition, and then to lose it altogether, because of the people around me who "magically" knew things that had no basis in reality at all, and expected that to give them influence over me. I was pressured to take seriously the "wonderful" intuition of others even when it had no discernible basis in reality, or was manifestly wrong. That did me a lot of harm. I do not live in that place anymore, and those very disturbed people no longer feature in my life.

When I started writing this book, I was still in a place of having rejected the impressions of my early life. I had become fiercely rationalist in self-defence, and disbelief had been my shield for years. All of my Paganism was pragmatic – based on the perceptible existence of the natural world. And so I left in the early parts of this book that which came from the first draft, and represented my opinion when I started writing. I did not believe, and I was not comfortable dealing with, the period of my life when belief had been possible, due to numinous experience that at the time, I had trusted. I had lost the ability to trust my own judgment across the board, needing to check far too many things with other people before I felt safe in acting. Again, this is not an unusual feature of abuse legacy. Healing so that I can trust my own judgment has been another facet of the process. Reclaiming my ability to trust my intuition and my sense of wonder has been hard, but I am getting there.

I have been working consciously and deliberately on re-enchantment, learning to trust my instincts again. Some weeks ago I dreamed I was in the company of a unicorn and it mentioned that virginity was never the issue. Innocence of heart was the issue, and that can be reclaimed. That I dream about unicorns now, rather than being locked into the same few horrible nightmares, says something about how far I have travelled.

Then came Druid Camp, in the Forest of Dean, above the Severn river, whose Goddess, Sabrina, had been so important to me when I was young. During my time there, I undertook a guided pathworking on Nodens, our local god of dreams and healing. The combination of place, people and relevance to me was irresistible, and I went.

There are many things I have coped with simply by learning to ignore them. Memories so awful that the only solution is not to bring them to mind. Bitter and painful things, and people who, when I think about them, still make me angry. So I don't think about them. There are holes from the loss of self and soul, and I have not found attempts at shamanic-style soul retrieval to be any use to me whatsoever. Just opening the door to places of loss and pain is really hard. I lay down on the grass in that workshop at Druid Camp, and I let myself remember that I had once been a true polytheist, capable not so much of belief, but of experience. I let myself feel the aching hole in my heart left by that loss, and I let a stranger's voice lead me into a pathworking.

There's a lot of trust in letting someone else guide you in a pathworking. Trust is one of the things I've been impaired in for some years now. Sometimes it's also the case that it's the things we give that we also find. I journeyed, and I remembered what it means to have a sense of sacredness, a real sense of connection, of being held in something bigger. I cried a lot, breaking another big taboo for me. I do not cry in public, I have not found it safe to do so. But, despite the presence of other people, some of them strangers, this was a safe space and I cried into it, for all that I had lost, for the wounded places inside me, for the need not to feel the grim isolation of depression.

Almost everything changed.

I started this book lost, living a hard life as a near hermit. I end it in a much softer place, with a community that holds me.

Around me are a group of people interested in the deities I once honoured, and I am slowly finding my way back to the sense of magical possibility I used to hold. I have hope and some scope for a future. Open wounds are starting to close over and heal. Broken parts of me are re-growing; not as they were before, but in ways that will work. So many of the things that I needed, and wanted, have fallen into place for me that I have a growing sense of abundance and good fortune. As previously commented, belief that the universe is not a hostile place and that there could be benevolent gods out there is easier to hold when you are not being kicked continuously by life.

Mostly prayer doesn't work. Except that to a degree I find quite disconcerting, mostly it has, and I did manage to walk out of hell, and I did not die, and there are good things. I am still not quite sure what to do with this, but *dear universe, I am bloody grateful.*

Thank you for sharing the journey.

Endnotes

1. *How to Pray*, John Pritchard, SPCK 2002, p104
2. *Ways of Praying*, John C Edwards, Family Publications, 1982, p2
3. *Judaism: A Very Short Introduction*, Norman Solomon, Oxford University Press, 1996, p68
4. *A Concise Encyclopaedia of the Baha'i Faith*, Peter Smith, Oneword Publications, 2000
5. *The End of Faith*, Sam Harris, Simon and Schuster, 2006, p44
6. *Benevolent Magic & Living Prayer*, Robert Shapiro, Light Technology Publishing, 2005, p25
7. *The Energy of Prayer*, Thich Nhat Hanh, Parallax Press, 2006, p24
8. *The Energy of Prayer*, Thich Nhat Hanh, Parallax Press, 2006, p39
9. *The Energy of Prayer*, Thich Nhat Hanh, Parallax Press, 2006, p35/36
10. *The Lightworkers' Circle Guide*, Wendy Stokes, O Books, 2010
11. *How to Pray*, John Pritchard, SPCK, 2002, p4
12. *The Philosophy of Religion*, Beverly Clack & Brian R Clack, Polity Press, 1988
13. *A Concise Encyclopaedia of the Baha'i Faith*, Peter Smith, Oneword Publications, 2000
14. *Opening to Spirit*, Caroline Shola Arewa, Thorsons, 1998
15. *Mystery Teachings from the Living Earth*, John Michael Greer, p69
16. *Islamic Thought: An Introduction*, Abdullad Sueed, Routledge, 2006
17. *Benevolent Magic & Living Prayer*, Robert Shapiro, Light Technology Publishing, 2005, p13
18. *Benevolent Magic & Living Prayer*, Robert Shapiro, Light Technology Publishing, 2005, p14

19. *The Magical Universe*, Stephen Wilson, Hambledon and London, 2000
20. *By Spellbook and Candle*, Melusine Draco, Moon Books, 2012
21. *Benevolent Magic & Living Prayer*, Robert Shapiro, Light Technology Publishing, 2005
22. *The Jain Path*, Aidan Rankin, O Book, 2006, p94
23. *Seeking the Mystery*, Christine Hoff Kraemer, Patheos Publishing, 2013
24. *Blood and Mistletoe*, Ronald Hutton, Yale University Press, 2009, p258
25. *Zen Druidry*, Joanne Van Der Hoeven, Moon Books, 2013
26. *King Lear*, Shakespeare

Moon Books invites you to begin or deepen your encounter with Paganism, in all its rich, creative, flourishing forms.